To Mark Our Place

To Mark Our Place

A History of Canadian War Memorials

Robert Shipley

Original
Photography by
David Street

**Foreword by
Pierre Berton**

NC Press Limited
Toronto 1987

For Mrs. Florence Smith
and all the other mothers
who lost their sons.
This book is their monument.

Cover design: David Shaw & Associates, Ltd.

Cover photograph: *Chester, Nova Scotia. Street.*

Previous page photograph: *Lichen pock-marks the face of the soldier on the monument at Ravenna near Georgian Bay in central Ontario. A possible foreign origin of the sculpture is hinted at by the collar, which is uncharacteristic of Canadian World War I uniforms, and the too realistic maple leaf badge. Street.*

Canadian Cataloguing in Publication Data

Shipley, Robert, 1948-
   To Mark Our Place

Bibliography: p. 194
Includes index.
ISBN 1-55021-014-9

1. War memorials - Canada.   2. Canada - History, Military.
3. Canada - Politics and government.   I. Street, David, 1947-.
II. Title.

NA9330.C3S45 1987   971   C87-094275-1

We would like to thank the Ontario Heritage Foundation, the Ontario Arts Council, and the Canada Council for their assistance in the production of this book.

New Canada Publications, a division of NC Press Limited, Box 4010, Station A, Toronto, Ontario M5H 1H8.

Printed and bound in Canada by John Deyell Company

CONTENTS

FOREWORD

In the summer of 1926, in my home town of Dawson in the Yukon, my father and some others arranged for the erection and dedication of an Egyptian obelisk known ever after as "The Monument." At its granite base was a brass plate containing a great number of names together with a note that said these names would live forever. Some of these names were familiar to us children for we knew other men and women in our town who bore those names. And so we came to understand that these were the names of those who had gone out from Dawson to fight in what we called The Great War and who had never returned.

On either side of the monument, standing in the tall grass of the little park like guardian sentinels, were two large artillery pieces on which we used to play. These were German guns. Somebody had arranged to have them brought all the way from Europe to this isolated community in the far north – a considerable feat and a remarkable gesture when you think about it.

At the age of six, then, I knew something about war. Each November 11 we gathered around The Monument in a ritual that was taking place in every community across the nation. I had no idea, of course, that other parents and other children were also making their obeisances to the dead and, in two silent minutes, thinking about the suffering and sadness that war brings. But the adults knew and this common rite, I think, played a part in what we call "national unity."

Canada, more than most countries, is a nation of Great War memorials. We have monuments to other wars and even to minor skirmishes, as Robert Shipley's carefully researched book makes clear. But most of our memorials have to do with what we once called The War To End Wars. I suspect that, along with Australia, we have more Great War memorials per capita than any other country. The cenotaph has long been a kind of small town rallying point where important visitors are directed for the ritual laying of a wreath. Its importance is

(opposite) Montreal sculptor Coeur de Lion MacCarthy cast three versions of this flamboyant statue for the Canadian Pacific Railway. This one stands outside Vancouver's waterfront station. Street.

signalled by the fact that it generally stands in the centre of a small park of square, so that the marble and granite figures are set apart from encroaching business blocks.

Why should this be? Why should a few hundred citizens in far-off Dawson have gone to the trouble of importing two cumbersome artillery pieces and several tons of granite to build an obelisk in Minto Park? Why are there more monuments, per capita, in the colonies than in the mother country? Why is Canada's Vimy Memorial arguably the most massive monument in France, commemorating as it does one of the briefest and least bloody of the Great War battles?

There is more than one answer. One, I think, has to do with pride. Canada entered the war as a colony, emerged as a nation. It suffered far more casualties than the Americans did in the First war and far more than it suffered in the Second, in spite of population growth. The Great War was a searing experience and also a turning point. We grew up as a result of that war; for the first time we came to understand that war is not gallant; it is hell. But if we lost our illusions we also lost our inferiority complex. Like the Australians we learned that we were the equal of any fighting nation on earth. That, really, is what we are saying with those captured guns in my home town: *"Look at us! We did it! We earned our place in the world community!"*

The monument says something else, of course. The names of the dead stand for the sacrifice as well as the futility of war – tens of thousands of them spread across the country engraved on sullen bronze. Here you can sense the lifeblood of the nation draining away, the flower of our youth scythed down, the promise of the future distorted. As this book suggests "War Memorial" is the wrong word; "Peace Memorial" serves us better.

It is good that this book has been written. The glue that helps to bind us as a nation is compounded of the folk memories of our triumphs and our tragedies. The outward signs of these common moments in our history are all around us in the buildings and the artifacts of the past. The cenotaphs that stretch from Dawson to St. John's are part of that historical texture. Mr. Shipley's work serves to remind us how rich that texture is.

Pierre Berton
Toronto, Ontario
April, 1987.

PREFACE

The question I have been asked most often during ten years of work on this book is: "How did you ever get interested in war memorials?" It's a perfectly reasonable question, but it is a bit like asking someone how it was they decided to get married. Even some of the very important things we do more or less happen without our making a specific decision to do them. Still, I can explain something about the origins of this book with the benefit of hindsight.

My father was in the army and I not only grew up in a military camp but eventually spent four years in uniform myself. An eye for military subjects was something I've always carried with me. Statues of soldiers standing on main streets fit into that category. Two of my other abiding interests have been travelling and drawing. While I was living in Nova Scotia in the mid 1970s these three interests came together. After weekend trips I began to notice that my sketch-books were filling up with pictures of seaside towns and villages that almost always included statues and crosses along with fishing boats and lighthouses. These monuments are not only common in the Maritimes but are features of most towns in the country. They are in fact so common, that while we are all aware of them, we generally take them for granted. I certainly did.

Then one day a crusty old seaman came up to me as I was drawing and started talking in that friendly way that east coasters have. "Boy, could I tell you some stories about that statue," he said—and he began to. I wrote down everything he told me at the bottom of the page and I suppose that is where and when I actually started this book.

It seemed that as a schooner captain in the 1920s this fellow had transported the statue I was then sketching down the coast from Halifax to the town of Chester. He told me that the superstitious sailors had been very reluctant to have the thing aboard. It was in a crate that looked like a huge coffin. In a way, I thought, it was a sort of surrogate coffin for all the men from that town who never came back from the wars.

It didn't take many trips to the library to find out that virtually no one had yet written anything about the monuments that are such a ubiquitous feature of Canadian communities. When I left the armed forces and set off on a career as a writer, there was a ready-made subject for me to tackle. But would anyone be interested? I concluded that it wasn't up to writers to decide what other people might or might not want to read. A writer has to follow his own sense of what is important. When he presents the results of his labour, others have to judge. After a long and not altogether easy process, this book has finally reached that point.

At best this study is a very general overview of a subject that has strong local and regional aspects. One of the things I hoped for in writing this book is that other people would be stimulated to do more detailed research than I have been able to in their own communities. Many of the ideas in the book will serve as guides and an illustrated glossary of terms has been added as an appendix to further help the local investigator. While the patterns in war memorials described in this book are quite strong, they are by no means uniform. Variations, new concepts, and even contradictions are bound to emerge from future work.

Thanking the people and institutions who have helped with such a large project as the researching, writing and publishing of a book is a tricky business. One doesn't want to make any serious omissions so I hope that everyone is included by category, if not by name. First in importance are my family and friends who have supported and encouraged me over the past few years. I knew that what I was doing was worthwhile, but they had to take my word for it. A grant from the Canada Council's Explorations Program, awarded in 1977, made a year of travel and research possible. Such grants are invaluable and perhaps too little appreciated. Several of my former professors at the University of Western Ontario, including A.M.J. Hyatt and James Reaney, were instrumental in helping me to secure funding and were generous with advice. I paid back one of these teachers, William S. Dale, rather dubiously by quoting him in the book and then disagreeing with his point of view. In spite of such treatment I am indebted to him as to the others.

Included in my research files are literally hundreds of letters that I received from interested people all over the country. They took the time to write and send information in response to notices that I placed in magazines and newsletters. Both the space in such journals as *Legion* and *Heritage Canada* and the responses from librarians, archivists, and amateur historians were invaluable. Herb Smale of Lawrencetown, Nova Scotia, for instance, collected pictures and material from all the communities in the Annapolis Valley and sent them to me. Once I actually began the trips that took me from coast to coast, the hospitality of Canadians everywhere was a joy in itself. Many people welcomed me into their homes and took time off work to show me the memorials in their areas. Bill Hall in Selkirk, Manitoba, and Ernie Gould of the *North*

Battleford News in Saskatchewan were just two of the many people who shared their time with me.

University of Toronto Press Editor-in-Chief, Ian Montagnes, contributed greatly to the development of the manuscript as did Malcolm Lester of Lester & Orpen Dennys. Ian helped me to secure funding from the Samuel and Sadye Bronfman Foundation, Koerner Foundation, and the Ontario Heritage Foundation for photographic illustration. Thanks are due to them and to Toronto photographer David Street for most of the excellent pictures that appear in the book. The Ontario Arts Council's Writers' Assistance Program contributed several grants that have helped me greatly. A grant from the Ontario Heritage Foundation assisted in publication. Lastly, I want to thank Janet Hamilton, Vivian Webb, Janet Walker, Noel Harding and Caroline Walker for their considered editorial advice.

Robert Shipley
St. Catharines, Ontario
August 1987.

INTRODUCTION
Your Children Will Ask

The very stones
cry out to us
too long
have we delayed . . .
        An anonymous inscription on the monument
        in the village of Douglas, Manitoba.

"LONDON SWELTERS AS MERCURY HOPS TOWARD TOP" was the headline in the *London Free Press* one hot, southwestern Ontario weekend in 1925. Another story on the same page described the unveiling and dedication of a war memorial in a suburb of the city. Two thousand people had gathered in Manor Park for the ceremony and a parade. Boy scouts, veterans, and the Manor Park Mothers' Club marched through the heat, along with local militia and detachments of regular troops from the garrison. Various dignitaries were also present, including London's mayor, George Wenige, and the reeve of Westminster Township, John Cousins.[1]

When everyone had assembled in front of the new monument, the Reverend William Beattie tugged a cord. The Union Jack fell away, revealing the white marble figure of a soldier set on a granite base. Reverend Beattie, who had been an army chaplain during the war, addressed the hushed crowd. "In the future," he said, paraphrasing the book of Joshua, "like the children of Israel, your children will ask, what is the meaning of these stones? (Josh. 4:6)"

By the 1980s that statue, dedicated in the sunshine in 1925, was a pathetic wreck. The soldier's rifle had long since been broken off by vandals, leaving the stone hands with nothing to grasp. In a macabre touch, the statue's severed head had been left lying on the ground beside the ruined memorial. The future that the Reverend Beattie talked about had arrived, along with the children of

(opposite) Our children pass by war memorials like this one in Mahone Bay, Nova Scotia, every day. What do they think about them? Street.

the original builders and their children's children. And looking at the tortured statue, or at the pages of the old newspaper, the question reverberates over the years: "What is the meaning of these stones?" (The monument has since been repaired.)

The scene of the memorial unveiling in Manor Park has been repeated over and over again in every part of the country. There are monuments to politicians, business leaders, and athletes, but Canada's past has been punctuated by bitter conflicts at home and overseas and it has been wars and rebellions that have given rise to most of our commemorative works. The process began at least as far back as 1759, when British soldiers marked the site of General Wolfe's death on Quebec's Plains of Abraham. Within the last ten years war memorials were still being built in places such as St. George's, Newfoundland, Atikokan in northern Ontario, and Qualicum Beach on Vancouver Island. The greatest number, however, were built, like the one in Manor Park, in the years after Canada's trial by combat in the First World War.[2] There are aspects common to all of these monuments but their story centres on the fervent years of the 1920s and '30s. Some of the memorials from that time were constructed while memories of trenches and telegrams of official regret were still fresh in people's minds. Others, such as the National Memorial in Ottawa's Confederation Square, were completed just in time for the reopening of hostilities in 1939.

Few memorials have yet been treated as badly by time as the one in Manor Park. But as the distance widens between the memories of the bulk of the population and the events that directly prompted the building of memorials, questions about their purpose and future become more critical. Growing up in the post-Second World War era, only vaguely or academically interested in wars long ago, and often thinking ourselves unaffected by them, younger Canadians have enjoyed the rare luxury of being able to pass judgement on their elders and neighbours without ever being involved in armed conflict themselves. My generation is apt to think that memorials, like the memories of war, are the sole property of those who were there. If that were so, then any significance monuments might have would not survive the present generation of veterans.

But the builders of monuments used stone and bronze and other lasting materials for their work. Did they want these commemoratives to testify to great victories, to serve their own vanity? It is hard to read what men said about the wars and then to imagine that they meant to erect reminders of such things in the centres of their towns. E. J. Spillett sent a letter home from the front during the First World War:

Dear Will,
   We take pride in the way we fix up our dead. Some battalions just pin the blanket around the corpse and send it in a shapeless parcel. Whenever possible we tie the arms folded across their breast, tie their

feet together and then pin the blanket around with the seam running down the centre of the body forming a cross with the seam running across the chest. Then we stitch it up and make a very neat job. The corpse is taken out at night to a cemetery about four miles behind the line.

I'm afraid I shall give you the horrors but this is war. There is no glory in it.[3]

The deaths had no less effect at home. Most Canadians of the time must have felt like the anonymous Edmonton woman who wrote to the mayor of that city when a memorial was being planned: "May I, a war widow, say that we who have lost our loved and best need no memorial or cenotaph to keep them in our memory."[4]

Monuments were not built solely for the benefit of those who actually experienced war or those who had been touched by its losses, although they have had a function for these people. In the central Ontario town of Arthur, the inscription on the monument at the main corner tells of a greater purpose: "In proud and honored memory of the men of Arthur whose names are inscribed opposite and who died for their King and Country this memorial has been erected so that after generations in this place may better know the cost to us of the preservation and continuance of British Liberty and Democracy."

The cenotaph in Vancouver is even more provocative. On two sides are carved the words, "Is it nothing to you, all ye that pass by?" Those who survived the war had suffered, but they felt they had learned some important lessons. They wanted to bequeath their hard-won wisdom to future Canadians. It is very much a fulfillment of the effort they began, therefore, for the children and the children's children to inquire after the meaning of the stones.

Canadian monuments have never been examined in a serious way. In 1908, long before the appearance of many of the memorials we see today, John George Hodgins, who was the Ontario Department of Education historian, issued a pamphlet entitled *"Canadian History as Illustrated in the Statues and Monuments which have been Erected in the Dominion."*[5] Although it was not much longer than its title, the text of the pamphlet proposed that historical societies jointly publish a picture book of monuments. That was as far as the project went. Hodgins's own collection of photographs is available only in the Archives of Ontario. In 1923 the Quebec government printed a two-volume work entitled *Les Monuments Commémoratifs de la Province du Québec.* Fifty years later a five-volume series compiled by Rodolphe Fournier, *Lieux et Monuments Historiques,* appeared in that province. The series included catalogues and descriptions of memorials, as did the November 1925 issue of the Montreal magazine *Municipal Review.* Yet neither said anything about the significance of monuments. A private collection of photographs now in the Archives of Manitoba in

Winnipeg, a 1937 article in the magazine *Canadian Homes and Gardens* dealing with the location of monuments, and a piece about Montreal's Nelson's Column that appeared in the English publication *Country Life* in July 1969, just about complete the list of attempts that have been made to document or discuss memorials in Canada.[6]

There are several reasons why this country's monuments have never been studied. The first is their age. They are, for the most part, simply not old enough to excite the interest of very many history buffs. One hundred years seems to be a magic number for Canadians. Buildings and objects over that age receive a great deal of attention, while the significance of items not yet so old is often overlooked. This can lead to a neglect that allows irreversible harm. In 1976 the Toronto Historical Board secured a grant from the Ontario Heritage Foundation to rescue some crumbling statues on an 1870 war memorial. A year later a modest appeal for federal government funds to help save a memorial tower in Duncan, British Columbia, was turned down. The Vancouver Island memorial was only fifty years old; in another fifty years it might not be there to repair.[7]

Definitions of what constitutes an antique, other than the one hundred-year test, are not much more helpful. Some suggest that "antiques are objects which cease to be made before the memory of living persons." If we hold off examination of memorials until no one is left who remembers their building, an incalculable amount of information will be lost. A man whose father operated one of the largest monument firms in the 1920s and '30s said that all of the old company records had been disposed of just a couple of years before I interviewed him. Another definition of antiques suggests that "simple disappearance from common use" makes an object an antique.[8] Monuments, if properly understood, however, may never cease having a function in our society.

The second impediment to an investigation of Canadian memorials has to do with the nature of the information available about them. The study of history has traditionally relied heavily on written sources. What makes up the bulk of "historical data" is what was recorded at the time, what participants in events wrote later, and the commentary of observers. Approaching Canadian monuments by way of documentary evidence alone gives the impression that there is not much to study. It has already been mentioned that there are few historical studies of monuments. Records relating to the origins of the monuments, such as memorial committee minutes, subscription lists, account books of monument firms, the memoirs of artists, and so on are almost non-existent. In the course of the text of this book, the readers will see how often information, such as people's full names, is missing. Government sources have their own particular reasons, as shall also be seen, for being almost totally silent on the subject.

But the shortage of written material about memorials does not necessarily preclude a deeper understanding of them. More and more those interested in the past have come to look beyond traditional sources in an attempt to see into

Many years after the event, these veterans of the Fenian Raids posed in front of the memorial that commemorated their exploits. The monument which stands on Queen's Park Circle in Toronto is now badly deteriorated. PAO.

the hearts and minds of people who have left few written records. One way in which this can be done is by interpreting the visual symbols and rituals of a culture.[9] Such symbols tacitly represent ideas and feelings that often cannot be easily expressed in other ways. Because public symbols are close to and in a real sense created by the people as a whole, they, along with participatory rituals, can be seen as a gauge of the sentiments of the otherwise silent multitude. Few symbolic objects are as common throughout the whole of Canada as war memorials. Few ritual observances have consistently involved as broad a spectrum of the society as Remembrance Day ceremonies. Together they form a unique window on some fascinating aspects of our history.

Because monuments have elements of design and are either ornamental or sculptural, art historians might be expected to have spent some effort studying them. Unfortunately, what little Canadian critics have said has been mostly derogatory. In the 1940s one wrote that memorial sculpture "defaced" public places in this country. He explained that the inability of the "man in the street" to understand sculpture accounted for the lack of interest in it.[10] In the 1970s *Artscanada* magazine said that sculpture was "without a strong cultural tradition on this continent."[11]

It is little wonder that, given attitudes like these, art historians and critics have contributed minimally to the understanding and appreciation of monuments in Canada. That hundreds of communities built memorials in the form of public sculptures in the first half of the twentieth century could be taken as a challenge to the assertion in *Artscanada* that no tradition of sculpture exists. As for the actual, as opposed to the figurative, "man and woman in the street," sculpture, unlike painting, is an art form they have seen often, when coming into town from the farm, for example, or on their way to and from the factory, office or school.

What many of our art critics have really been saying is that they do not feel that our monuments are worthy of study.[12] The styles have been imported, there is no distinctive Canadian expression, the monuments are just objects with which an artistically unsophisticated people cluttered their streets. But while it is true that no unique tradition of monument sculpture exists in Canada, the same could be said of Victorian architecture, colonial furniture, or impressionistic landscape painting. Would anyone claim, however, that the work of Emily Carr or A.Y. Jackson was not important simply because it was part of an art movement that reached beyond this country? Like early French Canadian armoires or the neo-Gothic buildings of the Canadian architect Frederick Cumberland, monuments in Canada were the local expression of international trends. Most of the stylistic influences on Canadian sculpture were imported but, as we will explore in the following chapters, these styles were themselves universal. Some of our monuments were copies of ones in other countries, but others were built earlier than those to which they might be compared. Nelson's

Column in Montreal was the first commemorative in the Empire built to honour the great naval hero. It predated the landmark in London, England, by thirty-five years. And while many of the artists who worked in Canada were trained elsewhere and immigrated, just as many were native Canadians who were self-taught or educated here. Some statues were imported into Canada, but several monument sculptures designed by Canadians are to be found in other countries. The statue of General James Wolfe that stands in his home town in southern England was sculpted by French Canadian Henri Hébert. Monuments in Canada may not represent an exciting group of state-of-the-art sculptures of their time, but they are certainly worthy of more study than they have been afforded.

The final and most problematic block to thinking about war memorials has to do with their subject matter. The poet Al Purdy says that a publisher once rejected a book of his because it dealt mostly with sex and death.[13] Similarly, there has been a rejection of thinking about war memorials because they appear to be about war and death. Neither of these is a topic that many people are comfortable with or even reasonable about. In a book about the sculptures on tombs in European churches, the author comments that "there is hardly any sphere of human experience where rationally incompatible beliefs so easily co-exist . . . as in our attitude towards the dead. Aboriginal fears and taboos of primitive man survive all around us (even in ourselves), and primitive rituals continue to be practiced, unbeknownst to those who do so."[14] This uneasiness concerning death, countered by the fact that the impulse for building cenotaphs and participating in remembrance rites seems to well up from our deepest instincts, is liable to make any analysis threatening to those who consider themselves primarily rational. Such analysis also runs the risk of offending those who feel that sacred issues should not be discussed at all.

The attitude towards war is no easier to cope with. It fluctuates from uncontrolled enthusiasm in times of perceived danger to widespread condemnation in periods blessed with prolonged peace. It would have been hard for student anti-war protesters in the 1960s to understand how their forerunners at the University of Toronto in the 1860s volunteered with at least equal zeal and formed the two leading companies engaged in the Battle of Ridgeway. It is just as hard for older Canadians, whose experience of war was the much vindicated struggle against Hitler, to accept that other conflicts lack a similar justification. To approach a topic that touches war during a peaceful if not altogether tranquil era like our own is to excite much the same reaction as discussing death and people's primal responses to it.

But Purdy goes on, in his story of the book rejected because of its themes, to say that the publisher, without meaning to, gave him "credit for knowing what's important – in both life and words on paper." He adds that in his writing "sex and death must always include love and life." So it is with war and slaughter, and with the monuments which are a peoples' response to them. Death and

On the base of the memorial in Sault Ste. Marie, Ontario are two bronze panels that tell us much about Canadian attitudes to the First World War; one shows men reluctantly leaving for war . . .

war are human experiences that are too fundamental and too frequent to ignore even though they are difficult to confront and understand. Furthermore, the memorials that seem at first glance to be only about war and death are really much more concerned with peace and life. While they speak of the dead, they speak to the living about things that are important in life. And while they were built after wars, mostly wars fought far away, they are products of this country and they are celebrations of peace. In 1922 the *Vancouver Sun* called a local monument a peace memorial. In 1931, in Toronto, the Shriners unveiled a statue at the Canadian National Exhibition grounds that was a monument to "Universal Peace." Memorials to peace, like peace itself, are part of the heritage entrusted to our time. We take peace for granted only at some peril. We allow the symbols of peace to deteriorate and let the ceremonial observances lapse only at the cost of diminishing our culture and thereby ourselves.

During the hundreds of years between the fall of the Roman Empire and the Renaissance, the people in Italy lived on top of the ruins of a magnificent civilization. They used ancient buildings as quarries for stone and burned sculptures to get lime for mortar. Then, at the dawning of a new age, they suddenly realized the incomparable value of the half-buried statues around them. They

. . . and the other pictures them grimly returning, bearing their dead. Shipley.

dug them out of the ground, raised them from the bottom of the sea, and re-stored them, not to temples to be worshipped, but to galleries where they could be studied and appreciated, and to public squares where they could inspire pride in and admiration for the past.

In Canada the reasons for not having tried to understand our memorials in the past, or for misunderstanding them now, need not persist. If we look care-fully at these pieces of our national and communal inheritance, we may well be rewarded with an enriched appreciation of our own unique society and country.

ONE
Incentive to Patriotism

. . . pour mon drapeau
je viens ici mourir.
  Octave Crémazie: "Le Drapeau de Carillon"

It was Christmas time in the year 1805. Deep in the interior of North America, Montreal lay ice-bound. Its citizens were not in a state of total hibernation, however, and the elite of the city had congregated at the fashionable Exchange Coffee House on St. Paul Street to celebrate the season. The gathering may not have been grand by Old World standards, but in the Montreal of that time it was considered a gala ball.

During the very height of these festivities there was a sudden interruption. "As the guests at the assembly were singing songs and drinking toasts in the supper room, a waiter hurried in with a New York paper and laid it before Samuel Gerrard." Gerrard was an Irish immigrant who would one day become president of the Bank of Montreal, and in 1805 he was already important enough to be the principal host at the Coffee House party. He now began to read aloud from the dispatch printed in the New York paper. There was immediate apprehension about Admiral Horatio Nelson who, the company learned, had met and destroyed Napoleon's navy off the coast of Spain the previous October. The great admiral was an extremely popular figure among the citizenry of imperial outposts such as Montreal, whose very existence depended on the strength of the Royal Navy. Those present were shaken to realize that while it was Nelson who led the fleet, the dispatch was signed by Admiral Cuthbert Collingwood, the third in command.

"I can never forget," William Henderson, another prominent Montreal businessman later wrote, "the electrifying effect of the news. While loud huzzas shook the very foundations of the building many . . . were shedding tears. The

(opposite) Some critics in 19th century Montreal felt the great Admiral Nelson should have been facing the sea instead of inland. But he was raised more to celebrate the maturing of the city that was the gateway to Canada than to commemorate naval victories. Street.

greatest of naval victories, clouded by the fall of the greatest of naval heroes."[1] Nelson was dead. It was reported by another man present that, "under the excitement of the moment, the chairman proposed that a monument should be erected in the city to the memory of Nelson. Ladies and gentlemen pressed forward to set down their names, so that in a few minutes a sufficient sum was subscribed."[2] One of those who contributed towards the fund of thirteen hundred pounds was a British army colonel named Isaac Brock.

In the early nineteenth century Montreal was not particularly impressive. Travellers from Europe found little about the place to recommend it. "The city," wrote one Englishman, "does not gain much upon closer inspection." "The streets are for the greater part most inconveniently narrow" and "the whole city appears one vast prison," said others.[3] Foreigners constantly complained about being "up to their knees in snow or to their ankles in mud."[4] But the citizens did not compare their city to the glories of Old World capitals. They were engaged in fashioning a civilization out of land that had barely emerged from the primeval forest. There were certainly no statues or monuments like those in Paris or Rome. Montrealers were just starting to build fine houses and churches and in time they would have waterworks, street lamps, constables, a city directory, and the other practical measures of civic growth. The news from Cape Trafalgar, even though it arrived late, was destined to play a part in changing the way Montreal appeared to others as well as the way it saw itself. Just four years after Nelson's death, the city could boast of having built the first monument in the Empire in his honour. The fifty-foot column rose to dominate the Place Jacques Cartier a full thirty-five years before completion of the familiar landmark in London's Trafalgar Square.

An English architect named Robert Mitchell was paid 958 pounds for the memorial design, which was modelled on the classic Doric order. Because of the structural limitations of the soft limestone available around Montreal, the local contractor felt it necessary to reduce the overall height of Mitchell's monument by ten feet. If the building material was unexceptional, however, the decorative work was not. The eight-foot statue of Nelson, as well as the ornamental work for the base of the monument, was made from a synthetic substance known as Coade stone, the current rage in Britain. The invention of Eleanor Coade and her cousin John Sealy, Coade stone was advertised as being "impervious to Frosts and Damps." It seemed the very thing for the Canadian climate, and the explorer Alexander Mackenzie was convinced by the promotion. Mackenzie and two other prominent Montreal merchants, John Gillespie and Thomas Forsyth, were in London on business for the North West Company and it was they who engaged Mitchell and authorized the plans for the monument on behalf of the Montreal citizens who had raised the funds.

Before it was shipped to Canada on the annual run of the Nor'Westers' ship *Eweretta,* the kiln-fired figure of Nelson was displayed in Coade & Sealy's London gallery. An old sailor is said to have come in and admired the likeness. He had served with Nelson and said, "This is really a grand figure of the gallant Admiral. I hope it is made of good stuff and that it will be as lasting as the world." John Sealy replied that there was nothing to fear on that score, "for his Lordship has been in a hot fire for a week without intermission." "You know something of the character of Nelson," cried the old tar, "for there never was a British officer who could stand fire better than his Lordship."[5] The statue still withstands the elements, though the base ornaments describing Nelson's victories and bearing the dedication from Montrealers have been retired to the museum of the Château de Ramézay in Montreal and replaced by replicas.

There were people who were no more impressed with Montreal after it had its first public monument than they had been before. They chipped away at the memorial verbally long before weather and bomb attacks by dissident groups had worked their mischief. Some said that the decision to build the column ten feet shorter than specified in the original design gave the whole monument indelicate proportions and made the figure of the admiral seem squat. They also pointed out that as a naval hero Nelson should have been facing towards the sea, not the northwest. But these criticisms seemed unimportant to most Montrealers, who were as proud of their memorial as they were of their burgeoning metropolis. One writer, commenting on the city's feelings about Nelson's Column, said that it was "lovingly described by virtually everyone."[6] In paintings, drawings, and prints depicting Montreal the column began to appear often. William Henry Bartlett, the English artist who toured the country between 1836 and 1838, included a view of it in his *Canadian Scenery,* published in London in 1842.

Not long after Bartlett visited Montreal he sketched another Canadian commemorative column. Brock's Monument, looking out over the Niagara River from the spectacular Heights above the village of Queenston, was also featured in his famous and still popular collection of prints. After making his donation towards the glorification of Nelson, Colonel Brock had gone on to become a general and to suffer a measure of glory himself. The column built in his memory could be seen by Niagara settlers from miles around. It is not by accident that both the Brock Monument that Bartlett sketched and the second one that later replaced it were also clearly visible from the American side of the border. While not in the centre of a city like Montreal's Nelson, the Brock Monument was just as important to the pride and growing sense of identity among the people of Upper Canada.

The nineteenth century was a precarious time for British North America and the uncertainty was most acute in the western province. Although the War of 1812 involved some questions of trans-Atlantic trade, the main area of friction that lead to hostilities was around the Great Lakes. And while some battles occurred elsewhere, most of the actual fighting was for possession of the terri-

The English artist, William Bartlett, captured the first Brock Monument at Queenston, Ontario before it was destroyed by terrorists. PAO.

tory that is now Ontario. Which side would win was by no means a foregone conclusion, and even after the war the United States remained a muscular and restive neighbour. Many colonists would have agreed with the historian J.C. Dent, who was still speculating about the country's ultimate destiny two generations after Brock's death. "The problem will be resolved in one of three ways:" Dent wrote, "by a general federation of the British Empire; by annexation of Canada to the United States; or by the establishment of Canadian independence."[7] Some people, then and now, believe that annexation to the United States might have been inevitable had not the Americans become impatient. After the War of 1812, and especially the Battle of Queenston Heights, everything changed. While annexation was still being discussed in Dent's time, it was moving steadily away from the realm of probability, until it would finally become unthinkable. Brock's Monument was one paragraph in the discussion.

In the fall of 1812, on the field where the monument would one day stand, the most psychologically important battle of the American invasion was fought. The war dragged on for two more years, but the failure of the powerful American force to win a decisive early victory was pivotal. Brock can hardly be credited with the victory at Queenston Heights, but what was more important to subsequent events was the death of the dashing general while leading a charge up the slopes. News of the far-off treaty that finally ended hostilities had barely reached muddy York (Toronto) in March 1815 when the Legislature of Upper Canada resolved to erect a monument to Brock. They voted to set aside one thousand pounds for the project.

Since Brock fell in the very early stages of the war and in an action that was later called "injudicious," we might pause to wonder why he was so revered.[8] Cynics would answer that war heroes who survive to become mired in ensuing events stand less chance of being loved than those who pass from us in their moment of glory. (Unlike Nelson and Brock, for example, Wellington the reactionary politician went a long way towards using up the credits amassed by Wellington the victorious general.) Statements from the time, however, reveal that Isaac Brock's real legacy to Upper Canada may have been more ideological than military. We need to remember that Brock was the civil adminstrator of the province as well as its army commander. "And whereas by the wisdom of his counsels," the legislative record reads, "the energy of his character and vigour with which he carried his plans into effect, the inhabitants of this Province . . . were inspired with fullest confidence in him and in themselves."[9] A feeling of community, a sense of being a distinct society, existed in Upper Canada after 1812. It had not really existed before, at least not outside Loyalist circles. Many residents of the province in 1812 were recent arrivals from Europe and even more had come from the United States in search of inexpensive and available land. They had no immediate attachment to the existing authority in Upper Canada, and their allegiance might never have galvanized had not a figure like Brock demanded it in time of danger and served as a focus for it in later years. The American invasion of Canada provided a lasting store of resentment and suspicion towards the United States that disposed people towards British protection and Canadian independence. Brock proved to be the perfect candidate for a hero around whom Canadians could rally. A memorial over his tomb would be the rallying point. A further six hundred pounds was voted by the Legislature in 1820 to complete the monument – and "sixteen hundred pounds was a large sum for the poor settlers of the day."[10]

When the Tuscan column was finished, it rose one hundred and thirty five feet over Queenston Heights. The observation platform, which was reached by way of an internal staircase, was well over four hundred feet above the level of the Niagara River. Thousands were present on October 13, 1824, when a long procession solemnly wound its way the seven miles from Niagara-on-the-Lake to the Heights, bearing the remains of Brock and his aide, Lieutenant-Colonel John Macdonnell. The bodies were interred in the base of the monument. Minute guns boomed from Fort George and from the American batteries across the river. Colonel James FitzGibbon, who had served in Brock's 49th Regiment and figures largely in the Laura Secord legend, had this to say about the occasion: "What I witnessed on this day would have fully confirmed me in the opinion, had confirmation been wanting, that the public feeling in the Province has been permanently improved and elevated by Sir Isaac Brock's conduct and actions while governing its inhabitants." Still dazzled by the sight of the monument and the procession, he went on to comment on the political orientation that Brock had left for his admirers. FitzGibbon said Brock's example had "done more towards cementing our union with the Mother Country than any event or circumstance since the existence of the Province."[11]

Not everyone in the colony was that enthusiastic about the British connection. While the echoes of 1812 were sufficient to keep the majority of Upper Canadians united in anti-republicanism, if nothing else, there were some who admired the American experiment and aspired to American-style institutions. Outspoken reformers such as William Lyon Mackenzie considered British administration oppressive and felt that movement towards responsible government in Canada was too slow. For Mackenzie and his partisans, the continued veneration of Brock as the defender of Canada against Americanism was simply a cover for depriving Canadians of greater democracy.

During construction of the first of the two Brock Monuments, Mackenzie demonstrated his opposition to what it stood for by having a copy of his anti-government paper, the *Colonial Advocate*, surreptitiously placed in the cornerstone. The column had reached a height of forty-eight feet before the plot was discovered. Work stopped dead until the offending journal could be removed. This method of sabotaging the monument was mild compared to what followed.

In 1837 Mackenzie and his followers joined their counterparts in Lower Canada in open revolt against the government. The rebellions were quickly quashed. Even before the revolt the printing press on which the *Colonial Advocate* had been printed was deposited unceremoniously on the bottom of Toronto's harbour. Having failed to bring about revolutionary change, Mackenzie and most active and known rebels found it advisable to remove themselves to the United States. They clashed with Canadian and British troops in a few incidents along the border, but after three years, calm had pretty well returned. At least that's what people thought.

Early in the morning of Good Friday, 1840, Alexander Lett, one of Mackenzie's erstwhile freedom fighters, crept back across the border. His target was Brock's Monument. "On the 13th of April, 1840," said the Honourable J.G. Currie of St. Catharines in an address in 1898 to the Niagara Historical Society, "I will not say how old I then was, I well remember – I heard a loud report which startled the whole village and country. Some base wretches from the other side, having an ill-feeling against our country, came over, placed powder in the monument and destroyed it, shivering it from top to bottom."[12] The column was left standing, but the stairs were gone and old prints show that a huge crack had been opened in the side of the structure.

"If it were intended by those who committed this shameful outrage that the injury should be irreparable, the scene which is before us, on these interesting heights, shows how little they understood the feeling of veneration for the memory of Brock which still dwells in the hearts of the people of Upper Canada."[13] This was part of what was said by Chief Justice John Beverley Robinson to an enthusiastic crowd which had gathered to plan a new monument. Lett's intent had certainly been to strike a blow against those who were pro-British or in favour of an independent Canadian state, but he found out what many terrorists after him discovered in similar situations. His action had the opposite effect from the one he had intended. Almost universal indignation was expressed across the province. A call went out from the lieutenant-governor, Sir George Arthur, for a mass meeting to be held at Queenston on July 30, 1840. The day was beautiful and sunny. From all parts of the province people came. There were militia officers, veterans, Highland pipers, and dragoons in burnished helmets. An artillery salute was fired. Every steamer on Lake Ontario was pressed into service. From Kingston, Cobourg, Toronto, and Hamilton they arrived, flags waving, and proceeded ten abreast up the Niagara River to the docks at Queenston. The H.M.S. *Traveller* brought up the rear. Over ten thousand people arrived on the Heights before noon. It was this assembly that John Beverley Robinson addressed. He represented the province's political establishment, which had a clear vested interest in promoting solidarity among the population. But also lending support on this occasion were many moderate reformers, among them, William Hamilton Merritt, champion of Upper Canada's commercial independence and a prime mover in the building of the Welland Canal. Robinson had been a young officer in the York Militia and was with Brock at the capture of Detroit in August 1812. Merritt had ridden into Queenston at the head of a troop of yeomanry just hours after the general's death in October of that fateful year.

At the high point of the mass gathering on Queenston Heights in 1840, an exciting spectacle captured everyone's attention. A young sailor from H.M.S. *Traveller* started to climb the damaged monument. Hand over hand he went up the lightning rod that stretched from the bottom to the top. The shattered stonework and the lightness of the rod made it a perilous journey. The huge crowd fell silent as they watched the young rating's progress. Once he had reached the top he felt in his pocket for a ball of twine. He let one end of this string drop down to his mates below and they fastened a Union Jack to it. The young sailor hauled up the flag amid tremendous cheers from the enthusiastic throng.

A resolution to erect a new monument was unanimously adopted. This time Parliament would not be asked for money from the public purse. Instead, funds would be raised by subscription. Both regulars and militia, officers and men, agreed to contribute a day's pay towards the memorial. Other donations followed until fifty thousand dollars had been collected.

Native peoples throughout the province contributed substantially to the fund and the testimonials that accompanied their donations remain the most eloquent statements of the outrage that was so widely felt.[14] "Our anger was great, when we were informed that the *Muck-o-Maws* (the Longknives) had, like wolves in the night, stolen into our Country and destroyed the Grave of a brave and gallant Soldier, Sir Isaac Brock," wrote Jacob Metegwaub, of the Saugeen River Band. "None but Cowards insult the Tomb of the dead: they are but dogs." Mackenzie's followers were not seen as Canadian rebels but as agents of the traditional American enemy, the "Longknives." "We have heard that the Longknife has destroyed, in the night, the Tomb which the brave had built to the bravest," came the message from the Chippewa on the St. Clair River. "That chief led us, as well as you, to victory. On that hill which we conquered, his blood was mingled with ours. Among our people the graves of the dead are sacred; the curse of the Great Spirit falls upon him who tramples on that even of an infant." The verbal curses, at least, continued to be piled on Lett. He was a "cowardly miscreant" who had committed a "diabolical act" and a "serpent with the double tongue" who had "polluted the resting places of the illustrious dead."

After this initial rush of interest, however, plans for the reconstruction of Brock's Monument seem to have languished for a time. It was 1842 before a circular went out from the monument committee giving specifications and announcing a design competition. Thirty-five entries were received in all, mainly from architects, and in 1843 the contract was awarded to Thomas Young, architect of King's College in Toronto. Young's design called for a huge obelisk in the Egyptian style. An obelisk would have been in keeping with American models of the time, such as Washington's Monument, built in the United States' capital in 1833, and the Bunker Hill Memorial, constructed in Boston between 1825 and 1843. But it was not to be. Long delays and difficulties over alterations were blamed for the eventual cancellation of Young's contract.

By 1849 the reconstruction of Brock's Monument was still not complete. It is impossible to say whether political events in that year had anything to do with a renewed push to finish the work, but a reformer named Peter Perry was successful in a by-election in the third riding of York. The chief excitement on the hustings was Perry's flirtation with the concept of continentalism. Because of this stand he became an instant hero to the group that supported annexation of Canada to the United States.[15] The rise of the continentalist faction in Canada no doubt recalled to the minds of some the need for reinstatement of a defiant Brock near the border.

By the 1853 anniversary of the Battle of Queenston Heights the new cornerstone was in place. This time the design was by Toronto watercolourist and architect John G. Howard, in association with William Thomas, another important early Canadian builder. Their monument, which now towers over Queenston Heights, was quite unlike anything that had been seen before in North America. The massive base consists of rough stones below with a smoother surface above. This contrast leads the viewer's attention upward to the carved ornaments and then to the huge fluted Corinthian column. At the four corners stand renditions of classical armour carved in stone. From the top of the one hundred and eighty four-foot monument a sixteen-foot likeness of Brock surveys the countryside. Most of the carving was completed by the Toronto firm of Cochrane and Pollock.[16]

The Rebellion of 1837 may have inspired plans to destroy old monuments such as the first Brock column, but the revolts did not immediately give rise to the building of many new ones. A few interesting memorials commemorating the civil strife appeared much later in both French and English Canada, but only one notable example was contemporary. Local tradition in the eastern Ontario counties of Stormont and Glengarry holds that the curious pyramid standing on an island in the St. Lawrence was built by militiamen who had been called up during the troubles of 1837. It seems their ingenious commander kept the underemployed troops busy on this prototype make-work project until they were disbanded.

Commemoration of the War of 1812, on the other hand, continued throughout the nineteenth and early twentieth centuries. Whether individuals supported continued strong ties with Britain and the Empire or dreamed of an

A war memorial or a make-work project? This mysterious structure is found in Eastern Ontario. PAC.

independent Canadian state, they saw 1812 as a metaphor for Canada's survival as a separate entity in North America. While the United States was digesting Louisiana and swallowing Texas, the Oregon Territory, and California whole, tourists in Niagara Falls could view the Lundy's Lane battlefield from a tower built for the purpose. The tower was replaced by a stone monument in 1895. In the same year the federal government erected a rough stone shaft at Allan's Corners, Quebec, south of Montreal. It marks the site where French Canadian militiamen and a band of native warriors under Lieutenant-Colonel Charles-Michel d'Irumberry de Salaberry, defeated the invading Americans in the 1813 Battle of Châteauguay. The first memorial to the legendary Laura Secord, who in June 1813 was supposed to have walked miles through the night to warn the British of an American attack, appeared in 1901 at Niagara Falls. An old cemetery that had been used by the Fort York garrison during the War of 1812 was discovered during turn-of-the-century building in Toronto, and a citizens' group erected a monument on that site called Victoria Park in 1907. The bronze half figure of a one-armed veteran was one of the earliest commissioned works done by Walter Allward, who went on to become a premier Canadian sculptor. The historian Ernest Cruikshank designed the 1812 War memorial erected at Fort Erie, Ontario, in 1909.

The centennial of the 1812 conflict brought with it a flurry of monument building. In 1912 a stone cairn was set up near Wardsville, in southern Ontario, where one hundred years before, English officers had ignored the tactical advice of woods-wise Canadian fighters and had lost the Battle of Longwoods Road. Just outside Hamilton, Ontario, at Stoney Creek, a commemorative tower was raised in 1913. The Battle of Crysler's Farm was also remembered by a monument built in 1813. It had to be moved in the 1950s when the new St. Lawrence Seaway flooded the original site and it now stands next to the reconstructed pioneer community of Upper Canada Village.

About the time the second Brock Monument was being completed in the 1850s, Britain and France found themselves involved in a war against Russia on the other side of the world. The Crimean peninsula in the Black Sea was about as far away from frontier Canada as one could imagine, yet events there had some small influence on this country. The Crimean War gave "The Charge of the Light Brigade" to popular mythology, via Lord Tennyson, and it gave memorials of sorts to numerous Canadian communities. When the French and British armies finally captured the Czar's naval base at Sebastopol they took some six hundred cannons with it. These were dispersed to the far corners of the Empire. It was hoped that in the parks of places such as Galt, Ontario, they would restore some of the lustre that Britain's martial image had lost during the war itself. The double-headed eagle of Romanoff Russia is still visible on these relics, though worn smooth by over a century of being climbed on by children. A deep mark on one of the Sebastopol cannons in London, Ontario, reminds us of the violence of war. It was clearly hit by a French or British cannon-ball during the seige, and we can hardly imagine the extent of the carnage it wrought among the Russian gunners.

Few Canadians were directly involved in that war so, beyond the novelty of the Sebastopol cannons, the impact of the Crimea on communities in this country was slight. An exception was Halifax. The presence there of both the Royal Navy base and a strong garrison attracted many young Nova Scotians to the imperial colours. Two local boys lost their lives in 1855 while serving with British regiments in the Crimea. It was in their honour that Haligonians erected the city's first public monument. In 1860 the garrison commander sent a detachment of soldiers to help the monument's designer, the sculptor and architect George Laing. The redcoats marched from the fortress which still looks out over Halifax to the wharves, where a quantity of red sandstone from quarries on the Northumberland coast of Nova Scotia and New Brunswick had been landed. They hauled the large blocks up to the old St. Paul's Cemetery in the centre of the city. Laing used some of the stones for the four steps that lead up to the base of the thirty-foot memorial. Others were used to form the pylons, vault, and pediment of the strong simple arch. "Parker" and "Welsford," the family names of the two men who were killed, and the numbers of their regiments were carved in the stone, along with the names of Crimean battles: Alma, Redan, Inkerman, Balaclava, and, at the top, Sebastopol. The soldiers must have strained under the weight of the fifteen-ton piece of freestone from which Laing carved the huge lion that surmounts the arch.[17]

By July 1860 this massive symbol of Britannic majesty was in place and the monument was dedicated amid much local excitement. The event was described in the wonderful doggerel of a Halifax bard known as "Will the Ranter of Craig Lee." The poem appeared in the 25 July edition of the Halifax *Morning Journal* in a column headed "Original."

> *Scenes ever shifting are before our view,*
> *Tragic and comic, always something new;*
> *The monument was an enchanting scene,*
> *It was a sight most worthy to be seen.*

Newspapers no longer treat us to such vivid reporting. For instance, Will the Ranter tells us who was there:

> *Never was such a gathering in that place,*
> *There seem'd but little or no empty space . . .*
> *The Governor and Admiral was there,*
> *And every one in his particular sphere;*
> *Grand master of free masons with his band,*
> *Soldiers, and volunteers was at command.*

In the days before loudspeakers such gatherings presented some technical difficulties:

> *The distant part which we took up our station,*
> *We could not hear the Reverend Hill's oration.*

Will completed his account with a word on the reception that followed the dedication.

> *The highland pipes play'd up a merry spring,*
> *And there in style was danced the highland fling;*
> *When done men broke out in rapturous cheers,*
> *Hurrah for Prince and Chearnly's Volunteers.*

The building of this arch was clearly an important moment for Halifax. Almost thirty years after its completion an elderly gentlemen of the city passed away. In his obituary, printed in the Halifax *Morning Herald* August 29, 1889, he was chiefly remembered as the stonecutter who had worked for Laing on the Parker-Welseford Monument.

Six years elapsed between completion of Halifax's Crimean War memorial and the summer of 1866, when the Fenian Brotherhood provided Canada's next commemorable military events. In the 1860s Canada and the Empire were nominally at peace, but Americans were killing each other by the entire regiment in the War Between the States. Thousands of Canadians, pursuing conviction or adventure, were involved unoffically in the American Civil War. No one knows for sure how many hundreds were killed and there are no memorials to them. For the ten Canadians who died defending their own soil in 1866, however, the situation is quite different. It was just a year after the southern Confederacy collapsed, ending the Civil War. Most of the Canadians came home, but many Irish-American veterans seem to have been at loose ends. Whether they were unemployed, had not had their fill of fighting, or were just fanatical, they congregated around a hare-brained Fenian plan to invade Canada.

The Fenian Brotherhood had been formed in the United States in 1858 by a man named John O'Mahony with the intent of raising money to help the cause of Irish independence from Britain. By 1865 there were two hundred and fifty thousand members and they set up a government-in-exile in New York City. At some point a plot was conceived in which the Fenians would capture British North America and hold it hostage until Britain granted freedom to the Emerald Isle. At the very least they hoped to divert British troops from Ireland. There was also some support for the scheme among Americans who still felt that continental domination was the "manifest destiny" of the United States. It was believed that should the invasion prove at all successful, Canada would inevitably slip away from British control and fall under American rule.

The Fenian raids into New Brunswick, Quebec, and Ontario met with stiffer opposition from the Canadian militia than the Irishmen had expected. As well, American government officials intervened in some instances and prevented the Fenians from even crossing the border. The sharpest clash that took place in Canada was at Ridgeway, near Fort Erie, Ontario, in June 1866. While the whole affair had a comic-opera flavour, it brought what war always brings to some, suffering and death. A monument honouring those killed was soon planned for the grounds of the Legislature in Toronto. By re-emphasizing the dangers of invasion from the south, the Fenians unwittingly provided the last impetus towards the confederation of the British North American colonies. By the time the monument was dedicated in 1870, the Canadian state had come into being.

Both contemporary newspaper accounts and the inscription on the monument indicate how it related to the prevailing mood of the time. "And now," said the *Globe*, on July 2, 1870, "the city of Toronto, the metropolis of Ontario, the pillar province of Confederation, records in monumental form the heroism of her sons, and interprets at once her grief and her pride." The inscription tells us that "Canada erected this monument as a memorial to her brave sons, the Volunteers, who fell at Limeridge, or died from wounds received in action or from disease contracted in service whilst defending her frontier in June 1866."

The *Globe* went on to emphasize the popular nature of the movement to build the memorial. "It was not erected by government or aided by government, and if today it commemorates the men of Ridgeway, even before they have mouldered into dust, it is owing to the people. The men who fought and fell and triumphed were of the people; so also is the monument." Sizable donations had come from as far away as Quebec City and the Sarnia, Ontario, area.

Toronto's Fenian Raid monument took a sort of Victorian wedding-cake form. The base is built of the same limestone used for Montreal's Nelson Column, while the multi-tiered body of the structure is the same red sandstone found in the Halifax Crimean War arch. The monument was designed by Robert Reid of Montreal, who also sculpted from Italian marble the allegorical and soldier figures that adorn it.

This Russian Crimean War cannon is displayed in a Montreal Park. Street.

In the century before the First World War, the impulse to commemorate incidents and outstanding individuals from the past posed potential problems for French Canadians. While they lived under British rule and were expected to be unflinchingly loyal, more than a few of Quebec's many folk heroes had made their mark fighting against England. Building monuments to record Quebec's history was one method used by groups like the Institut Canadien and the Societe Saint Jean Baptiste, which were charged with fostering French Canadian pride and traditions. Their efforts took various forms and elicited various degrees of acceptance or suspicion from their English-speaking compatriots.

In 1858, in Montreal's Côte des Neiges Cemetery, "a lofty column of grey limestone" was "erected to the memory of those who either lost their lives or suffered punishment for the part they took in the uprising of 1837-38."[18] In the twenty years that had elapsed since the rebellion much water had gone over the Canadian political dam. No one in authority was prepared to admit that armed revolt was justified – after all, this was not the United States – or that the rebellion had directly precipitated changes; but the grievances had been acknowledged and reforms, attributed to purely constitutional methods, had come. The popular wisdom of the day had allowed the "rebels" to be promoted to "patriots." Nothing much could be done for the patriots who had been killed in battles or executed, but a measure of vindication had come to those who had returned after deportation. During the time the Côte des Neiges monument was being planned, Dr. Wolfred Nelson, who had led the patriots at the Battle of St. Dennis in 1837, was the mayor of Montreal. Nelson was one of the few people of English background to have been involved in what was largely a revolt of the French Canadians against British domination, but his later career in city politics did demonstrate a degree of reconciliation. It is interesting to note that while most of the rebels listed on the column were French, both the builder and the designer, whose names are shown as L. Hughes and T. Fahrland, were not.

In 1860 the Société Saint Jean Baptiste wanted to celebrate the centennial of the Battle of Ste-Foy, fought on April 28, 1760, near Quebec City. It had been one of the few French victories during the War of the Conquest, though it had not altered the final outcome. The society erected a monument that consisted of a Doric column on a high base. Four mortars were mounted on the corners of the base and a statue surmounted the column. The monument was designed by a Frenchman, Charles Baillarge, and the statue was a gift from Prince Jerome Bonaparte, cousin of Emperor Napoléon III. Perhaps to avoid controversy the Société Saint Jean Baptiste diplomatically called it the *Monument Des Braves,* a name that denoted the gallant and worthy on both sides. The inscription bears the names of both François de Lévis and General James Murray, the French and English leaders at the battle.

Valleyfield, Quebec, possesses another creative approach to the question of suitable French Canadian heroes, one that commemorates people whose claim to fame lay entirely outside the Canadian context. During the nineteenth century, the *Rissorgimento,* a movement to bring the various states in Italy under one national government, slowly took the remnants of temporal power away from the Papacy. The year 1868 saw the beginning of the last act in that drama. The Pope appealed to devout Catholics from outside Italy to come and help him defend his shrinking worldly kingdom. Hundreds of young French-speaking Quebecers joined a regiment of volunteers and a monument to the members of the Papal Zouaves from the area south of Montreal was erected in Valleyfield.[19]

One of the first individual Quebec heroes to be remembered by a monument was a man eminently acceptable to both French and English-speaking Canadians. On June 1, 1881, a statue was unveiled in front of the town hall at Chambley. Montreal sculptor Philippe Hébert, who incidentally was among the Quebec Zouaves who had gone to Italy, had created an imposing likeness of Lieutenant-Colonel Charles de Salaberry. De Salaberry was a loyal officer in the British service, a spirited, duel-fighting adventurer, and the victor at the Battle of Chateauguay in the War of 1812. He had been a great friend of Queen Victoria's father, the Duke of Kent. At the same time he was part of a long line of outstanding French soldiers and a distinguished member of Quebec's seigneurial class. The Marquis of Lorne, who was then the governor general of Canada, spoke in French at the dedication. He said the statue was "raised in no idle boasting, but with a hope that the virtues shown of old may, unforgotten, light and guide future generations."[20] The Marquis of Lorne clearly felt that fighting for England was a particularly high virtue to which French Canadians should aspire. A statue of de Salaberry also stands at the end of a bridge near Valleyfield.

Fifty-eight years after the uprising of 1837, and thirty-seven years after the first memorial to the patriots, a statue of Dr. Jean-Oliver Chénier was erected in Montreal at the corner of Craig and St. Denis streets. Chénier was a fiery leader who had been killed at the Battle of St. Eustache in December 1837 and was the first of the French Canadian rebellion principals to be honoured by a statue. One of the *Front de Liberation du Québec* cells involved in the kidnappings that precipitated the October Crisis of 1970 also commemorated Chénier by using his name, but in 1895 the patriots of 1837 were not yet identified as proto-separatists.

Another monument that stands in Montreal's Place St. Louis could be called a quasi-war memorial.[21] It seems to represent some strong and unspoken French Canadian sentiments. Octave Crémazie was a nationalist poet whose themes often harkened back to a time in Quebec when French martial glory was great.

> And all the old Canadians reaped in war
> Rise also from their funeral couch, to view
> The dear fruition of their highest
> dream.[22]

In this poem he mused upon the return of French power. The incident that inspired the verse was the arrival, in 1855, of a French warship in Quebec. It carried Prince Jerôme Bonaparte, on an official visit, and it was during his stay that he offered the statue for the *Monument des Braves* at Ste-Foy. The memorial to Crémazie, built in 1906, includes the statue of a dying soldier holding a flag. It bears the inscription: "*Pour mon drapeau/je viens ici mourir*," lines from Crémazie's poem about Montcalm's defence of Fort Carillon (Ticonderoga).

A story about the dedication of a statue to the great Marquis de Montcalm himself reveals the nervousness that some of these monuments could cause among English Canadians. October 16, 1911, was the date set for the ceremony in Quebec City. The commanding officer of the 9th Regiment, Les Voltigeurs de Québec, a French Canadian militia unit, requested permission to parade his men, with arms, at the event. Although it was within the authority of the senior commander at Quebec to allow this, he turned to his superiors in Ottawa for a decision. Ottawa quickly approved the parade and wrote back to the colonel commanding the 5th Division in Quebec. The letter ended: "As it is not understood why an application of this nature was submitted to Militia Headquarters for approval, I have to request that you will be good enough to state your reasons for so doing."[23] An equally prompt reply came from the local commander in Quebec City:

> I have the honour to state for the information of the Minister in Militia Council, that I was perfectly well aware I could authorize a parade, and that it was not exactly the permission of the Department which was sought but in my opinion the question was one coming within the general policy of the Government, and was therefore submitted for their decision and approval. The turning out of a Canadian Militia Regiment composed entirely of Canadians of French descent, and in honour of a General who died in arms against British Troops, is not an ordinary every day affair.[24]

It was not an ordinary affair and in many places it would not have happened at all.

Commemorating pre-conquest heroes enjoyed a vogue in Quebec around the time of the First World War. The great legends from the struggle between New France and the native peoples were replete with suitable characters: the young Madeleine de Verchères, for example, defending the farm and her siblings from the onslaught of Iroquois warriors. A statue of Madeleine, by Philippe Hébert, stands in the town that bears her family name. Dollard des Ormeaux was another hero from the same period. In 1660 an Iroquois attack was shaping up on the Ottawa River near Montreal. Dollard took a small band of men and occupied an old fort barring the way to the settlement. All the Frenchmen were eventually killed, but according to legend, their spirit so discouraged the Iroquois that they thought better of an assault on the town. Monuments to Dollard can be found in Parc Lafontaine in Montreal, in Asbestos, and at Carillon where the fabled battle took place. (This Carillon is a town on the Ottawa River and is not the Fort Carillon of Montcalm fame.)

While commenting on a ceremony being held at one of these monuments in 1923, an English-Canadian army officer wrote: "These exploits of Dollard, which we read of in our school days, appeal to English Canada as much as they did to French Canada, although I doubt if French Canada knows it."[25] It is doubtful that this enthusiast understood the full implication of the memorials in question. There was considerable bitterness in Canada on both sides of the conscription issue during the First World War. Many French Canadians volunteered, but there was much feeling that the war in Europe was not Canada's affair. Charges that French Canada lacked fighting spirit must have stung, and the Dollard and Verchères monuments are part of the response. They say that French Canadians are not afraid of fighting and have a rather long history of service where their homeland has been threatened.

Tension was not always characteristic of monument building in Quebec. One of the very earliest memorials was erected in Quebec City in 1828. It was the design and suggestion of an officer of the British garrison named Young, but the committee that raised the money included both Judge Jonathan Sewell and Judge Jean-Thomas Taschereau. The monument was an obelisk commemorating Wolfe and Montcalm, and the inscription on it is written in Latin rather than either French or English: *"Mortem Virtus Communem Faman Historia Monumentum Posteritas Dedit,"* "Their courage gave them the same death, history gave them the same fame, and posterity the same monument." In 1907, in Toronto, the *Globe* said this commemoration of both victor and vanquished by the same monument had no parallel in the world. The same year an astonished visitor to Montreal witnessed the unveiling of the city's Boer War monument. Three thousand soldiers marched through the streets to the sound of orders given in both languages. "This is one of the most unique sights I have ever seen. British and French, the old-time rivals of the world, marching shoulder to shoulder. Why, Montreal contains within itself the essence of universal peace. Two races living as one in peace and fellowship. It is wonderful."[26]

The building of monuments took a somewhat different course outside Quebec in the decades before the First World War. As the country expanded westward, the new Dominion government in Ottawa sought to establish its jurisdiction over freshly acquired lands. Before long it began to meet opposition from those who already inhabited the great plains. Native peoples and Métis felt they should have more say in the future of the West. Louis Riel, an educated and almost messianic Métis leader, emerged to head the resistance. In 1870, at Fort Garry, and in 1885, in Saskatchewan, there erupted armed confrontation and finally pitched battles between native and Métis bands and government troops.

History's opinion of the Red River and North-West Rebellion continues to be revised. At the time, for Canadians from Winnipeg and the East, it was all a legitimate part of our particular version of imperial expansion. Most of the troops involved on the government side were militia from the Maritimes, Quebec, Ontario, and Winnipeg. Memories of the battles and the men lost in them were soon fashioned into monuments.

One of the first of these memorials was completed just about fall-fair time in Ontario, in 1889. The front page of the Toronto *Globe,* on September 4 of that year, said, "Port Hope . . . Industrial Exhibition opens today. Space awarded exhibitors is crowded. Entries better than expected. The Premier and Sir A. Caron will unveil Williams' statue at 11 o'clock and formally open the Exhibition at 2 P.M. The town has put on its holiday attire for the occasion." To be dedicated in the presence of Sir John A. MacDonald and many others was a larger-than-life figure of Lieutenant-Colonel Arthur T. H. Williams. The sculptor was Hamilton MacCarthy of Toronto. An address from the memorial committee, printed in the Toronto *Globe* September 5 1889, was read to the crowd:

> The object of this Association was declared to be the erection of some monument to the memory of our departed townsman which should be national in character and as such worthy of the Dominion and which should be placed in the public square in the immediate vicinity of the Town Hall and the new Post Office in the town which gave the Dominion the courteous, kindly, gentleman, the gallant Christian soldier, the true-hearted, unselfish patriot whose virtues it was proposed thus for all time to hold up for the admiration of future generations.

Arthur Williams had been the member of Parliament for the area and was the commander of the battalion from eastern Ontario that was sent to fight in the North-West Rebellion. He was one of the militia leaders who, ignoring the over-cautious instructions of General Frederick Middleton, the Englishman in charge of the expedition, had brought a quick end to the fighting at Batoche, in Saskatchewan. Williams died later of disease, but his monument depicts him, hatless, sword in the air, leading a charge.

Statues in St. Catharines and Ottawa are more sedate. The Ottawa figure has been moved from its original location on Major's Hill to the park behind the National Arts Centre. It shows a soldier in the traditional pose of mourning: "resting on arms reversed," in the military parlance. On the stone base are bronze plaques bearing likenesses of two Ottawa men killed in the rebellion, privates John Rogers and William Osgoode. The St. Catharines monument features another moustachioed soldier standing at ease. It commemorates Private

A rare sight in 19th century Canada: this girl's school cadet corps poses in front of the North West Rebellion Monument in St. Catharines, Ontario. PAO.

Alexander Watson. A bronze female figure holding the olive branches of peace surmounts the North-West Rebellion monument in Toronto's Queen's Park. Parks in Peterborough, Ontario, and Russell, Manitoba, have fairly simple stone commemorations of local participants in the suppression of the revolt. Perhaps the largest memorial to the 1885 rebellion is the fifty-four-foot classical column that stands beside Winnipeg's City Hall. The monument is called "The Rebellion Shaft" and one wonders if it was named by the Métis? It has a statue of a soldier on top, and with its ornately carved base is slightly taller than Montreal's Nelson memorial.

As for the rebels in the West, they are not widely celebrated with monuments. A modern and somewhat abstract and controversial statue of Louis Riel stands by the Assiniboine River near the provincial legislature in Winnipeg. Poet and playwright James Reaney speculated that there might be some significance in the fact that Riel is behind the parliament buildings, almost totally surrounded by a concrete wall, while Manitobans placed their statue of Robbie Burns out in front facing the main streets.[27]

The South African or Boer War, 1899 to 1901, was the last struggle of the nineteenth century in which Canadians were involved. It gave rise to a greater

*One of the focal points of Halifax's beautiful
Victorian gardens, this fanciful commemorative
fountain is said to be surmounted by the
portrait sculpture of a local hero. Street.*

number of memorials than had any previous wars. Monuments appeared not only in larger places such as Saint John, New Brunswick, Montreal, Ottawa, and Toronto, but in smaller cities such as Brantford and Sarnia, Ontario, and even in some towns and villages such as Newtonville, Newmarket, and Southampton, Ontario. One of the largest statues in the country, and the only Canadian war monument showing a mounted soldier, was made after the Boer War for the booming new city of Calgary.

Historical perspectives on the South African conflict have changed over the years. It appears now to have been the first modern instance of a large imperial power, Britain, locked in an unequal guerrilla war with a small state. Similar conflicts subsequently occupied the French in Algeria, the Dutch in Indonesia, the Americans in the Philippines and Vietnam and the Soviets in Afghanistan. All these wars were essentially unwinnable in the long run and caused division at home. But the changing view of history does not alter how people reacted at the time. In 1900 many Canadians saw fighting for the empire in South Africa as a noble cause.

Halifax built not one but two monuments after the Boer War. One is of a bronze, pith-helmeted, and moustachioed soldier who holds his rifle over his head and looks out over the harbour from his spot beside the Nova Scotia legislature. The sculpture and the scenes in relief on the base were the work of the same Hamilton MacCarthy who created the Port Hope, Ontario, statue of Lieutenant-Colonel Williams. The Boer War was to make MacCarthy a very busy man. The other Halifax monument is an ornate iron-work fountain which stands in the city's public gardens. The figure of a Canadian Mounted Rifleman on top of a mythical, water-spouting fish and exotic birds is said to be a likeness of Billy Pickering, a well-known athlete from Halifax who went to South Africa after his adventures in the Klondike Gold Rush. Photos of him in his uniform were sent to the Macfarlane Iron Works in Glasgow where the statue was made. In later years, when Pickering took walks from the nearby Camp Hill Veterans' Hospital, people said he was the only Canadian who passed by his own monument every day.

A great amount of excitement surrounded the erection of these monuments in Halifax, as it did elsewhere. When a memorial was first suggested in October 1900, the city's newspapers talked of little else. Different headlines in the Halifax *Herald* of October 13, 1900 read: "A Memorial for Nova Scotia's South African Heroes," "Evidence of a Nation's Love and Gratitude," "Their Memory Would Be Honored For All Time To Come," "Nova Scotia Should Set Example." The papers carried lists of those who had already donated money. There were drawings of elaborate proposed designs. Also in the *Herald*, there were numerous letters to the chairman of the memorial committee: "What should be the logical sequence of our lusty cheers in Halifax on Pretoria night? Let us build something in honor of our brave boys that will endure for aye. To honor the brave and furnish incentive to patriotism in our children's children."

The feeling that fighting for the Empire was an admirable cause found expression everywhere. A turn-of-the-century county history in Ontario, referring to the local Boer War memorial in Cayuga, said, "In these days Haldimand has noble sons, worthy of their fathers of days gone by."[28] The inscription on Granby, Quebec's memorial says it was built "both as an abiding mark of appreciation of their loyal devotion to duty in the cause of Queen and Country and also as an incentive to the young men of Shefford to be ready to emulate their noble example of patriotic self-sacrifice whenever in the cause of right and justice they may be called upon to serve his most gracious majesty the King."

While the Halifax paper, *Bluenose*, on October 13 in the excitement of 1900, could editorialize about how we were "Canadians all but Britons more," something beyond total identification with Britain began to emerge with monument building after the Boer War. The scene in London, Ontario's Victoria Park on May 29, 1912, was right out of a Stephen Leacock story. Thousands of men in straw boaters and women in fashionable bonnets crowded the grounds. When the local 7th Militia Regiment arrived, it looked at first as though they were not going to get anywhere near the object that was the centre of everyone's attention. The Duke of Connaught, fourth son of Queen Victoria, and governor general of Canada, arrived with his wife and his daughter, young Princess Patricia. When the unveiling cord was pulled, however, the dramatic moment fizzled. The covering caught on the statue's arm and much unceremonious prodding and poking with poles was needed before the sculpture was completely visible. This was not the first snag in the history of the monument. Most of the speakers on that spring afternoon knew what had happened in the preceding years but avoided mention of it. A fire during the time that Montreal sculptor George

Hill was still working on the monument was the feeble excuse now given for the ten years it took to complete the statue.

It had been 1902 when London's mayor and council sanctioned the idea of a Soldiers' Memorial. A local chapter of the Imperial Order Daughters of the Empire (IODE) took on the task of raising money. The city fathers made some donations from the municipal budget, but the rest was made up from band concert proceeds and contributions from school children. Eventually, ten thousand dollars had been collected.

Things went along smoothly after the decision in 1902 to build a monument until the question of design was considered. The venerable monarch, who had given her name to the age and to London's park, passed away about the same time the Boer War ended. The idea of including a memorial to the late queen along with the Soldiers' Memorial was suggested. Very quickly two factions developed within the IODE group planning the monument.

It was an affront to Queen Victoria to place her on the same monument as a common soldier, said one side. The scheme that this group opposed called for a plaque dedicated to the queen to be placed on the base of the soldiers' statue. Proponents of the plan tried to side-step the criticism. They explained that the late ruler was such a magnanimous person that she would never have been insulted by having her image placed below that of one of her loyal defenders, even a mere colonial. It was no use. Tempers began to run higher and hotter. One irate lady phoned a reporter and insisted that there were only two types of women in London. His ears perked up but it turned out that she was referring to what she called "Loyalists" and "Disloyalists." The first group were those she agreed with and the latter were the others. Among the comments made at the time there were some amusing ones: "Some women say that a statue of Her Late Majesty would not be artistic. Well, I believe in Loyalty before art."[29] More often the women's comments were very eloquent and expressed such sentiments as a desire for a strong national character for Canada that would still serve the Empire.

The dispute became so bitter that the local IODE Chapter was expelled from the national organization for its internal disputes and public displays of emotion. Both sides engaged lawyers and prepared to fight for their idea of what the proper patriotic attitude should be. The women were chagrined when the final decision was taken out of their hands and made by a committee of prominent businessmen. In its completed version a female figure offers a laurel crown to a striding soldier above her. Whether the soldier represents the new independent Canadian spirit and whether the female figure is the incarnation of the Victorian Empire is up to the viewer to decide.

By the time more momentous events overshadowed the South African War there were several more monuments in Canadian communities. Some were large and impressive like the statue in Quebec City, with its extremely heavy-

Calgary has the only war memorial in Canada depicting a mounted soldier. Shipley.

looking bronze flag. Others were more modest, such as Charlottetown, Prince Edward Island's version of the Royal Canadian marching to Pretoria. The bronze plaque in the middle of a rose garden in Windsor, Ontario, is small but beautiful in its setting. Canning, Nova Scotia, and Woodstock, Ontario, were among places where portrait busts of local men killed in South Africa preserve the look of turn-of-the-century Canadian men.

At the beginning of the nineteenth century most communities in the string of colonies that was to become Canada were scarcely more than clearings in the wilderness. The season by season struggle for survival against both natural and human forces consumed much of people's energy. As the years passed, however, there were more cultivated fields, more permanent buildings to take the place of the first rude habitations, and there was the time and inclination for settlements to begin developing into real towns and cities. The building of public monuments was one of the elements in that progression from trading post or crossroads to urban maturity.

As they beautified and landscaped the streets and parks around them, Canadians searched eagerly for subjects to memorialize. In Woodstock, Ontario, the square in front of the town hall received a fountain dedicated to a local politician who had become provincial highways minister. Kincardine, Ontario, has a sundial that remembers the service of a dedicated community doctor. In Carbonear, Newfoundland, a monument commemorates the heroism of the town's postmaster who died trying to save the burning mail depot. In St. John's, Newfoundland, and Saint John, New Brunswick, memorials were raised to would-be rescuers who drowned trying to save friends.

One of the most notable incidents of heroism occurred in Ottawa in the winter of 1901. A man named Henry Albert Harper perished in the frigid waters of the Ottawa River along with the young woman he was attempting to rescue. She had fallen through the ice while skating. Bert Harper's closest friend and associate was the future prime minister, Mackenzie King. In a "naked outpouring of anguish such as he would never permit himself again," King wrote about his friend's virtues, "in a tortured little book."[30] *The Secret of Heroism* was dedicated by King "To My Mother."[31] At the time King was Deputy Minister of Labour and reasonably well connected in Ottawa circles. Largely through his efforts a statue of the archetypal hero, Sir Galahad, was erected on Parliament Hill in honour of Harper.

In spite of the appearance of these personal and civil monuments, however, it was important military events at home and abroad, and the heroes that emerged from them, that were the bench-marks in the struggle that shaped the colonies into a nation-state. They most often provided the inspiration for memorials. While monuments were a phenomenon of urban growth, there was more to them than that. From the first one commemorating Nelson to those honouring the Boer War soldiers, they expressed a sense of patriotism and of service to the state, chiefly in the context of British imperialism. For many Canadians the British connection continued to be a pillar in the structure of their identity. French Canadians, starting with their first monuments, asserted a distinct national pride. An equally definable feeling was something that developed more slowly in English Canada. From Brock through the other 1812 memorials to the Fenian Raid commemoratives, the distinction was mainly expressed in terms of surviving pressure to become part of the United States.

By the time of the Boer War, Canadian identity was taking a more positive and outward-looking form. There was always an assumption on Britain's part that all sections of the Empire, whether self-governing or not, would aid her in any conflict. There was still plenty of blind support for Britain, but more and more Canadians were coming to feel that the country's actions should be dictated by its own best interests. When England became ensnared in South Africa, Prime Minister Wilfrid Laurier did not automatically commit Canada. A compromise was reached that allowed imperial enthusiasts to ship themselves off to the Transvaal but did not compel anyone to do so. Those who did leave the country were the first Canadians to act on behalf of the new Dominion in the international sphere. The monuments from the time celebrate that independent entry into world affairs.

Local distinction showed up as well. The soldier on Winnipeg's Rebellion Shaft is not dressed in just any period uniform. His greatcoat and fur hat are well suited to the legendary weather of Portage and Main. In Calgary, the Stampede city, it is hardly accidental that the only mounted Canadian soldier is found. Local building materials were used where possible and artists from within the country were preferred.

Increasingly the subjects of commemoratives were local people. We may think of Wolfe, Montcalm, Lévis, and Brock as Canadians, but they were in fact British and French. Some of the home-grown heroes such as Dollard and Lieutenant-Colonel Williams were giants. Many others were more ordinary. They were stretched to fill hero's garments because people wanted to feel that others like themselves could rise to confront difficulties bravely. Dr. Chénier was shot when he jumped out of the window of the burning church at St. Eustache. William Knisley, whose name appears on the Boer War Monument at Cayuga, Ontario, was wounded when he stopped in the midst of an inglorious retreat to help a friend. Walter Price of Granby, Quebec, died of enteric fever, not in South Africa, but in England in 1900. They were heroes because we needed them to be.

The nineteenth century did not end when the midnight bells rang on December 31, 1899. Neither did it finish when its first lady went to her rest in 1901. In Canada it lingered like ice on the shaded side of a hill in spring. The real end of the age came in the hot summer of 1914. There were still only a handful of towns and cities that had built public monuments. The years after 1914 were to see every community in the country rudely pulled from innocence. Lundy's Lane, Batoche, and Paardeburg would seem like skirmishes as people painfully learned the place names of Flanders and Picardy. Where a few heroes had once marched, ghostly battalions would pass on a scale not dreamed of in the worst Victorian nightmare. Canada's identity would be purchased with blood abroad and written in stone at home.

1914-1918

TWO
Citizens of all Classes

. . . but whether they believed it or not
they acted as though they did
and built the monument
– that seems important
   Al Purdy: "One Thousand Cranes"

A Canadian soldier with his muddy boots still on lay asleep in a half-destroyed Belgian house. It was an hour before noon, November 11, 1918. Suddenly he "awoke with a start." About him "hung the silence of a tomb."[1] "Quietness reigned where before noise and turmoil of war had prevailed."[2] The conflict in which millions had perished was over. Between 1914 and 1918 over six hundred thousand Canadian men and women had traded their civilian clothes for uniforms. That was almost one person out of every twelve in the young Dominion. Now counted among the uncountable dead were sixty thousand Canadians. The United States, with ten times the population of Canada, had lost fewer.[3]

If the 1918 Armistice brought a cherished silence to the weary soldiers on the front, it had the opposite effect back home. The news of November 11 served to reanimate the country's voice. The *Calgary Herald* reported that the screaming whistle of a Canadian Pacific Railway (CPR) locomotive had been the first notice of peace in that city. According to the Toronto *Globe*, November 12 1918, "Other whistles followed suit, the news spreading like wildfire, and in a few minutes there was a bedlam of bell ringing, whistle blowing and cheering." Crowds surged onto Yonge Street in Toronto waving flags, stopping streetcars and cheering "in unison with that joyful noise." On the main streets of rural towns the Kaiser was burned in effigy. The Toronto *Globe* continued its description of the momentous day: "The silent and invisible herald of peace was encircling the globe in the form of a wireless message that Germany had signed the

(opposite) The dates of the World Wars and the Korean conflict are the only inscription on the National Memorial in Ottawa's Confederation Square. Street.

armistice . . . . How that silent message found instrumental and vocal utterance, and the invisible was made visible will remain the loftiest landmark in Canada's national life, and will be a story that those who live through it will tell with zest to their grandchildren."

The survivors of the fighting returned, some to a semblance of normal life, some to live out their days in veterans' hospitals. Peacetime life resumed. More immediate concerns captured attention as months and then years came to stand between the people and the horrible war they had endured. But after the public euphoria had receded and the tears of personal loss had dried, something of that "instrumental utterance," that "invisible feeling made visible," remained in the monuments the nation built.

Writing about the effects of the war in eastern Ontario, W.S. Harrington remembered that:

> during the four years of conflict . . . . the all-absorbing passion for victory often prevented full expression of sympathy with the silent suffering of those who were bravely bearing a heavy burden, because of the loss of sons or relatives . . . . But scarcely had the armistice been signed when a wave of sympathy swept the land in their behalf, and an almost universal expression of grief and sorrow was heard . . . The depth of thanksgiving for peace was only equalled by the desire on the part of all classes . . . to erect to the memory of those who had fallen some fitting token of respect and reverence.[4]

Almost all places in the country had borne their share of the loss. Inscribed on the memorial in Ripley, Ontario, are the names of 260 local people who served in the armed forces in the First World War. Thirty-three of them did not return. The population of the village and surrounding township was just under 3,000. In Granby, Quebec, the monument shows the names of 129 local residents who took part in the war. Of those, 17 were killed in action or died of wounds or disease. Granby's population in those years was about 2,000. In industrial towns and cities the figures were slightly higher than in rural communities. Of the 10,300 people in Galt, Ontario, at the time of the Great War, some 1,800 enlisted. The memorial in Galt records the loss of 241 soldiers. There were few people in the country who were not touched personally. Mayor Charles Simms, quoted in the Victoria *Daily Colonist* of November 13, 1921, summed this up at the dedication of the memorial in Courtenay, British Columbia, when he said, "There is scarcely a person in the throng before me who has not lost someone, son, brother, husband or father."

The desire for fitting tokens of respect took hold of people's imaginations. Peace was only nine days old when a letter from the town council of Longueuil, Quebec, to the Minister of Militia made reference to *un monument que cette*

Ville à l'intention d'ériger sur un de nos parcs publics à la mémoire de nos soldats qui sont tombés au champ d'honneur."[5] The frontier village of Bjorkdale, Saskatchewan, had a memorial stone bearing the names of local men killed in the war just seven months after the Armistice. A few months later, still in 1919, a statue was erected in front of the Young Men's Christian Association (YMCA) building near the coal mine pit-head in Canmore, Alberta. It was the late 1920s before permanent memorials were completed in Montreal, Winnipeg, and Peterborough, but soon after the war temporary monuments were in place in those cities. The one in Peterborough stood in the fair grounds and consisted of a riderless horse on a pedestal.

Most Canadian victims of the 1914-1918 holocaust had "passed out of the sight of men by the path of duty and self-sacrifice" on some stretch or other of the wretched piece of geography known as the western front.[6] The carnage along this swath of no-man's-land was so great that it took years to find and rebury the bodies of the dead. Almost twenty thousand Canadians were never found and have no known graves. Many of the names of those forever missing are carved on memorials in Canada, and from those monuments we can get some idea of just how confusing the war was. So concentrated was the fighting that it even took time before the names of the various battlefields were clarified. The man who had commanded the Canadians in Europe, Sir Arthur Currie, wrote to Army Headquarters in September 1924. He had seen plans for a memorial being built at the University of Western Ontario in London. He noted that the names of battles to be included on a bronze plaque were wrong. After Currie's note Major-General James MacBrien wrote from Ottawa to district commanders suggesting that they keep an eye on memorials being erected in their areas. Major-General H. D. B. Ketchen replied from Militia District No. 10 that often the first hint he got that a memorial had been built was a few days before the unveiling when he was asked to attend.[7] If there were mistakes they were by then already carved in stone.

It seems that people's notions of how to divide up the amorphous war came partly from places that veterans remembered, partly from newspaper accounts, and, to some extent, from the military terminology that was used. When the names "Lens" and "Hill 70" are recorded on a memorial, such as the one in Merritton, now part of St. Catharines, Ontario, the same battle is really being referred to twice. Lens was the nearest town to the battlefield and the name veterans might have recalled, while Hill 70 was the designation on the generals' maps for the ridge where the fighting actually took place. Similarly, the memorial in Fredericton, New Brunswick, lists Canal du Nord and Boulogne Woods as separate battles. In fact, they were part of a continuous engagement fought on September 27, 1918.[8] The Somme, on the other hand, was a series of actions that dragged on for months, yet it rates only the same mention on monuments as these other battles. General Currie felt that these misnomers did not accurately describe the war in which so many had fallen. Requests for the federal government to verify lists of battles to be used on memorials were still being received as late as 1928 when one arrived from McCallum Granite Company, "architects and builders of memorials of merit," in Kingston, Ontario.

Figuring out where individuals and units had fought was also difficult. In the 1920s and '30s memorial committees from Melville, Saskatchewan, Verdun, Quebec, and Cornwall, Ontario, wrote to Ottawa asking in what battles the men from their towns had been involved.[9] They were told that drafts of troops from every part of the country had been broken up to reinforce the casualty-ridden units at the front. Because of that fact, men from virtually everywhere in Canada had been present at each of the major battles. It was therefore rare for a particular battle in the First World War to have specific significance for one location in the country. Newfoundland is one exception. It was not part of the Canadian confederation at the time and troops from there fought with the British army. Beaumont Hamel is a French village that gave its name to an action that occurred on the first day of the epic Battle of the Somme. On July 1, 1916, the Newfoundland Regiment (later to be designated the Royal Newfoundland Regiment) was almost wiped out in half an hour. Six men from the town of Placentia alone were killed that day. Their names are among thirty-six on the monument in front of the town's Catholic church. The story was the same all over Newfoundland.

The inscription on the monument in The Pas, Manitoba, attempts to get around the problem. It reads simply, "Ypres to Mons." Ypres was the first battle in which Canadians were involved and Mons was the last. In a final ironic twist that again exemplifies the futility of the First World War, the last Canadian battle took place in the very same spot where the British and Germans had first clashed in 1914. When the 49th Battalion from Edmonton marched into the Belgian town of Mons on the morning of November 11, 1918, it had merely arrived back at the place where the conflict had begun. But figuring out who fought where and naming and spelling the battles correctly was only incidental to the building of memorials since they are not so much records of confusing events as expressions of profound emotions.

Some fairly elaborate memorials were completed within two or three years of the war's end. The streets of Lunenburg, Nova Scotia, climb sharply uphill from the old shipyards and wharves of the waterfront. One block of the main street was closed off after the war and made into a park. Since January 1921 a stone soldier has gazed out from among the trees, past masts of fishing boats and over the sea. Forty-one local men, whose names are carved on the base of the statue, never recrossed the ocean to Lunenburg. The statue of "a soldier standing in an attitude which indicates readiness and even eagerness to go forward, typifying well the response which was made by men of the district," was unveiled in Rimouski, Quebec, on September 21, 1920.[10] Almost a year before

The First World War had not yet ended when this temporary monument was built at Ganges on British Columbia's Saltspring Island. BCA.

that a monument had been completed in the Notre Dame de Grace section of Montreal.

A general wave of enthusiasm for building monuments swept the country immediately after the Armistice, but thoughts of memorials had not always waited for peace. The Princess Patricia's Canadian Light Infantry was the first unit from this country to reach the front and it did not arrive until after Christmas 1914. The First Canadian Division was not in action until February 1915. But as early as December 1914, the Canadian Club of Vancouver had petitioned the British Columbia government, asking that the old Court House Square be set aside for some form of memorial. Not a single person in a Canadian uniform had yet been killed. In Vancouver and elsewhere, however, there was some premonition of what was to come. Early in 1917, as casualty lists mounted, the Belleville, Ontario, Women's Red Cross wrote to Ottawa to ask for the use of a plot of land in front of the city's armouries. At Ganges, on British Columbia's Saltspring Island, a temporary monument was actually built before the end of the war. On the grounds of the Canadian National Exhibition in Toronto there were wartime displays of trenches in connection with recruiting and Victory Bond drives, as well as a massive temporary monument sculpted by Francis Loring called "Canada Sending Her Sons To War." In April 1917, Middleton and Eastman Company, Wholesale Granite Merchants of Hamilton, Ontario, wrote to army headquarters in Ottawa. Eastman asked for "a cut of a private soldier with such equipment as would go with a statue."[11] The company evidently had customers already. They explained that, "as we have a large wholesale trade through the northwest and Ontario and will have more inquiries for this, [we] would like to have it right."

Most of the movements aimed at erecting monuments did wait until after the war before they really got started in earnest. Building efforts began in various ways. Surrounded by a fancy border, the following notice appeared a year after the war on the front page of the November 6, 1919 edition of *The Signal* in Goderich, Ontario:

> All citizens interested in the fund
> for the establishment of a Soldiers'
> Memorial in Goderich are requested
> to attend a meeting to be held in
> The Menesetung Canoe Club
> Rooms, in the Masonic Temple on
> Wednesday Evening November 12th 1919
> at 8 o'clock for the purpose of
> instituting a general canvas [sic] of the town.

The historic town of Goderich looks out over Lake Huron from the top of a high clay bluff. The Huron County Court House stands in the hub of eight radiating main streets and the park that surrounds it was a perfect site for a monument. In the weeks that followed the November 12 meeting the paper told how several dozen people had gathered and from their numbers elected a committee to oversee the memorial venture. It was learned that the Canoe Club had already collected $2,494.12 and in doing so had deducted none of its own expenses. Those present at the first and subsequent meetings voted to invest the money in Victory Bonds until it was needed and to continue collecting funds for the memorial.

The Vancouver Canadian Club had considered a memorial from the very start of hostilities in 1914. The civic authorities in Vancouver had also set up a team to study the idea, and in 1923 the two groups met in the Metropolitan Building and formed a twenty-four member committee that set as its purpose:

1. The erection of a memorial to those who fell in the Great War;
2. Such memorial to be erected on Victory Square; and
3. The memorial not to cost more than $15,000.00.[12]

Often things were less formal. In the resort and fishing town of Chester, Nova Scotia, a public meeting was held one summer night in a schoolhouse. Present were both permanent residents such as Cottnam T. Smith and summer visitors such as J. Massey Rhind, a sculptor from New York. The meeting "considered ways and means – principally means," Rhind said, of building a memorial.[13] The suggestion for a monument in Napanee, Ontario, was first made at an Armistice celebration held in the town's armouries. After that, "the local press and various organizations discussed the matter freely, and after some months public opinion took definite form in the appointment of a committee to consider the different propositions that had been presented."[14] An extract from the *Red Deer News,* December 18, 1918, said, "All loyal citizens in the Central Alberta district are urged to give this movement their hearty support." The paper went on:

> The movement that has been under consideration since the signing of the armistice respecting a memorial to the heroes of the Central Alberta District took concrete form at a large gathering of the Great War Veterans' Association and representative citizens held at the City Hall Monday evening. The resolution unanimously adopted at the meeting was as follows:
>
> WHEREAS a very large number of brave men from the Red Deer Dominion Riding of Central Alberta did join the colours to fight for King and Country and the cause of Freedom in the world-war 1914-1918, and
>
> WHEREAS to the grievous sorrow and loss to the community, many will never return, having made the supreme sacrifice on the fields of Flanders and other battlefronts, and
>
> WHEREAS it is fit and proper that the glory of local heroes, sacred and green in our minds today, shall live forever by visible memorial and tribute
>
> BE IT RESOLVED that a strong committee from this representative meeting be appointed to co-ordinate with the Great War Veterans' Association, and other good and loyal citizens, for the purpose of arranging ways and means of raising and handling a Memorial Fund, and the form of such memorial.

The early 1920s were days of high unemployment and difficult times. The roads were not paved in rural Canada and few people had cars. Mass media was a weekly paper and news was passed by word of mouth in the grocery store, barber shop, and at church. The 1921 census shows that an even one half of all Canadians still lived outside urban areas. It was not always easy to get these memorial efforts under way. In Chatham, Ontario, the original memorial adherents were described later by the committee secretary as "an insignificant few" who "resolved that though years go past while life shall last we would remember."[15] In

Beeton, a village in the country north of Toronto, "the non-attendance of the general public" at the opening memorial meeting in 1921 was attributed "to the inclement weather which prevailed throughout the forenoon and which had the appearance of continuing on into the night."[16]

Even when the idea of building a memorial was widely endorsed and enthusiastically pursued the unforeseen could complicate matters. The population of the small Ontario community of Ayr was only seven hundred but one hundred men enlisted. A large proportion of those who joined up, 23 in all, were lost. Judging from the response to a public meeting called by the reeve in 1921 it was obvious that the people wanted very much to erect a monument. Then a fire destroyed the town's major industrial plant, putting most of the men out of work. Collecting the necessary funds and concentrating on the project became very difficult.

Nevertheless, the drive to build memorials went on. Just two years after the fire in Ayr a cross, which still stands in the centre of the main street, was unveiled. A memorial gate marks the entrance to the fair grounds in Beeton. By 1923 the work begun by the "insignificant few" in Chatham, Ontario, had grown into a movement large enough to build a monument that cost fifteen thousand dollars. The secretary of the memorial committee, Arch Skirving, said "they quietly persisted in their efforts, for the word failure was not in their lexicon."[17]

Various groups organized memorial committees. The Canoe Club in Goderich, Ontario, and the Canadian Club in Vancouver are just a couple of examples. In Medicine Hat, Alberta, it was the Rotarians who got things rolling, and in Weyburn, Saskatchewan, it was the Young Fellows' Club. In Lacombe, Alberta, and Blind River, Ontario, Lest We Forget Societies were formed. At the head of the Great Lakes the Fort William Women's Patriotic Society took on the memorial project. In a great many other communities the initiative also came from women's groups. The Queen Mary Needle Work Guild was responsible for the monument in Granby, Quebec, while Danville, Quebec, had its memorial movement started by a knitting club. Devlin, Berwick, and St. George, Ontario, along with numerous other places, owed their monuments to the Women's Institute. Most active of all the women's organizations in the period after the First World War were the redoubtable ladies of the Imperial Order, Daughters of the Empire (IODE). Among the communities where they started memorial committees are Moncton, New Brunswick, Wainwright, Alberta, Carberry, Manitoba, and Quyon, Quebec. Thirteen of the twenty-eight members of the committee in Red Deer, Alberta, were women, and they represented not only the IODE and the Women's Institute but the Women's Christian Temperance Union, the Eastern Star, church auxiliaries, and the local Council of Women. The signature on the minutes of the Red Deer committee meetings is that of a "Mr. Snell," indicating that none of the women accepted the job of secretary.

Women's direct involvement as members of the armed forces during the wars was not widely acknowledged before this monument was erected in Winnipeg in 1976. Shipley.

The prominence of women in memorial movements after the First World War was part of the growth of women's involvement in all aspects of our society. The war had brought about great changes, not least of which was the increased need, in the absence of so many men, for women's labour and skills in the workplace and in volunteer organizations. Because women had been called upon to perform so many non-traditional roles, and had proved themselves capable, they gained confidence and, for those who needed it, justification for demanding an increasing share of recognition, responsibility, and independence. In 1924 an army officer in London, Ontario, answered a letter from Margaret MacIntyre, the secretary of the IODE memorial committee in the nearby town of Strathroy. He addressed it to "Mrs. MacIntyre," and in a prompt reply was told pointedly that it was "Miss" MacIntyre. Besides filling factory, agricultural, and other full-time jobs, women had also shouldered much of the social and relief work during the war. A woman wrote to Ottawa about a proposed monument in Florence, Ontario. She gave a list of the number of socks, pajamas, and pillowcases that the local women had made and sent overseas. These had all been shipped through a larger centre and her concern was that the village would not get proper credit for its contribution. Not all women's energies were directed towards working and knitting socks, however. There had been an interest in more deadly war work. An erroneous news report during the war intimated that there were not enough machine guns for Canadian troops in the trenches. Patriotic women's groups started the "Machine Gun Fund" and thousands of dollars were collected before embarrassed officials cooled the ardour with assurances that the government was supplying sufficient weapons to sustain the rate of slaughter on the western front.[18]

When the war ended, the drive and organizational momentum of women's groups was strong enough to complete the fight for suffrage and prohibition. In many places it transformed itself into efforts to erect memorials as well. These ventures must have been considered important. The enthusiasm with which women worked, however, was not always proof against criticism and difficulty. The IODE in London, Ontario, was accused of trying to take over and dominate work on the city's memorial. These women were not only daughters of the Empire but daughters of the IODE women who had fought the ten-year debate over London's Boer War Monument. Things worked out in the end and all was forgotten, but the results of a mistake that arose in Oxford, Nova Scotia, were more permanent. The Women's Institute had worked long and hard in Oxford towards the day when the memorial would be unveiled. Finally, the moment came. The town gathered in the park on the main street, but when the Union Jack fluttered to the ground, the crowd was staring at the back of the statue. The stone soldier, depicted in the posture of one charging forward, was charging down a side street with his heels towards the business section of Oxford. There was no money left in the fund for the expense of turning the figure around, so there it stayed, a handsome if misplaced memorial to the men of the town who had been lost in the war.

The dedication of women's groups in initiating memorial movements was matched only by the efforts of the Great War Veterans' Association (GWVA). The GWVA was the largest of several veterans' organizations that were originally formed after the First World War to provide ex-servicemen and women with a collective voice, and to represent their pension, medical benefit, and re-settlement interests in the public and political arenas. In 1925 Field-Marshal Earl Haig, who had commanded all the British and Dominion forces in the war, attended the national convention of the GWVA. At his urging most of the veterans' groups joined a year later to form the Canadian Legion. The Legion had a less official function as well. It had grown in part out of the deep comradeship that had sustained servicemen through the horrors of the trenches and the hardships of long separation from home. From this more personal and social side came the desire to commemorate lost friends.

Although established clubs and organizations were often responsible for taking the first steps towards erecting memorials, the movements usually spread out to include a wider range of citizens. At the first meeting of the memorial committee in Edmonton in November 1927, Colonel F. C. Jamieson moved a vote of thanks to Mrs. E. N. Higginbottom of the IODE. The women of that group had been working for two years collecting money before joining with others to form a general committee. The expanded organization included, among others, Mayor A.U.G. Bury, Campbell Young, of the Old Timers' Association, W. M. Evans, of the Disabled Vets, the Anglican Bishop, and G. W. Waistell of the Workmen's Compensation Board.[19]

South of Edmonton, in Red Deer, Alberta, the memorial committee expanded from the original GWVA organizers to take in representatives not just of the many women's groups, but also of the United Farmers of Alberta, the Masons, the Alberta Natural History Society, the Sons of England, the Horticultural Society, and the Board of Trade.[20] The committee in Guelph, Ontario, was made up of members from the Men's and Women's Canadian Club, the Trades and Labour Council, the YMCA and YWCA, the Teacher's Association, the Foresters, the Rotarians, the Independent Labour Party, City Council, and the Knights of Columbus. The committee secretary was George Drew. He went on to become premier of Ontario and national leader of the Progressive Conservative Party but in the early 1920s he was always pictured in his wartime major's uniform. Writing one day in the *Guelph Daily Mercury,* under such a picture, Drew stated that "it was felt this committee was entirely representative of the general feeling of the city, as it included organizations which embraced every group in the community."[21] A printed souvenir from the dedication ceremony of the Brantford, Ontario memorial says that "in 1921 the need for an appropriate commemoration of those who died for their country was generally realized and citizens of all classes united in the formation of the Brant War Memorial Association."[22]

The varied occupations of the committee members are a further indication of the breadth of community involvement in the movements to build monuments. Besides George Drew, the lawyer and politician, just about every type of person served on committees. Charles Huestis worked for the Mann Axe and Tool Company in St. Stephen, New Brunswick. Rev. R. J. McCarten was a clergyman in Priceville, Ontario. A. E. Gardener of Manor Park, Ontario, was a foundry worker. "Grandpa" Medhurst farmed in Foremost, Alberta, and Ned Bently ran a garage in Summerland, British Columbia.

In scattered instances an individual or particular family, rather than a general committee, undertook the building of a monument. The Denison dynasty of Toronto erected its own family memorial in the cemetery at Weston. In another cemetery on the Muncey Indian Reserve, near London, Ontario, there is a statue dedicated to Arnold Logan. The young member of the Muncey Band was killed in action in France at the age of nineteen. Along with such family memorials there were a few family-sponsored monuments in public places. The bronze statue of a handsome, kilted officer that stands beside the town hall in Amherst, Nova Scotia, is a likeness of Captain Leon Curry. He was said to have been the first graduate of Acadia University to fall in the First World War. His

This statue of Captain Leon Curry which stands in Amhurst, Nova Scotia, is one of the rare protraits on a Canadian memorial of the post World War I era. Street.

parents, Senator and Mrs. Nathaniel Curry, donated the statue for the town's memorial. In Morewood, Ontario, a village near Ottawa, a huge box arrived by horse-drawn sleigh one winter night in the 1920s. It had been hauled up from the nearest railway station at Chesterville and contained a life-sized granite statue of Captain E. J. Glasgow, late of the 154th Battalion, Canadian Expeditionary Force. The portrait had been purchased for the local memorial by Captain Glasgow's brothers. In Almonte, another Ottawa Valley town, the Rosamond family owned one of the mills. They commissioned retired doctor-turned-sculptor Tait MacKenzie to create a likeness of their son Alexander, who had asked that a statue of him be erected if he were killed in Europe. The sculpture now serves as the local memorial. It is thought to have been so lifelike and exact that the bereaved mother asked MacKenzie to alter the face so as to spare her feelings. In Wallaceburg, Ontario, an aging and sonless mariner named Captain J. W. Steinhoff gave the money for a memorial figure. Unfortunately he did not live to see the monument completed.

Even though such monuments, or at least the statues on them, were sponsored by individuals or families, the dedications were still to all the lost soldiers from the community. The Morewood inscription reads, "To all those who offered their lives in humanity's defence in the great war of the nations." Alexander Rosamond's name is included in alphabetical order among the others on the Almonte memorial. In most of these cases there was a need for community participation in building the memorial that went beyond the donated art work. R. J. Graham of Belleville, Ontario, had made a great deal of money during the war in the food-processing business. He set out to provide the town with a monument, but it is remembered with some bitterness that relatives of the deceased soldiers were then asked to pay ten dollars to have the names of their loved ones included in the inscription. The sculpture that was supposed to surmount the Belleville memorial never arrived. Some said that it went down in a torpedoed ship during the Second World War. A cross was finally added to the top of the monument in 1978 as a community project during the city's centennial year.

One of the first things that many memorial committees did once they were formed was to turn to the government for some advice and direction. In the years after the war the letters streamed into Ottawa. They came from the town clerks, businessmen, housewives, veterans, and members of Parliament who made up the memorial committees. They came from large cities such as Montreal, from rural towns such as Shaunavon, Saskatchewan, and from small villages such as the Huron settlement of Jeune Lorette, Quebec. People wanted to know what sort of monuments should be built? Would the government provide designs? Was it true that Ottawa planned to pay part of the cost of memorial halls? Replying to one of these letters in February 1919, an assistant deputy minister of defence said that "the matter has, to some extent, been considered." When the Honourable Robert Anderson, MP for Halton, wrote in March 1919 requesting information on the government's intention regarding monuments, the answer he got was that, "although this subject has received a certain amount of consideration, the department has not adopted any definite policy."

Suggestions as well as inquiries were made about the government's position on memorials. Prime Minister Sir Robert Borden was away at the great Peace Conference at Versailles in 1919 so Frank Wickson, president of the Royal Architectural Institute of Canada, wrote to Sir Thomas White, the Acting Prime Minister: "It seems to us most desirable that the groups of people who are endeavouring to express their gratitude and respect to those who have given their lives for the sake of liberty, should be assisted to do it in a way that will be artistically worthy of our country. There will almost inevitably be a tendency on the part of manufacturers to exploit these opportunities, utterly regardless of the aesthetic result."

Wickson went on to say that the architects thought the government should appoint a commission to approve memorial designs. Naturally, members of his institute would be glad to serve on such a commission. On its odyssey through Ottawa offices the architect's letter crossed the desk of Brigadier-General E. A. Cruikshank, director of the army's historical section at the time. Cruikshank was concerned that the architects might come to dominate the selection process. According to their plan, members of their organization would be submitting designs that their colleagues on any commission would be approving. Cruikshank thought their proposal "scarcely judicious."[23]

Next into the act was the colourful member of Parliament, Major-General Sir Sam Hughes. Hughes is a much maligned figure in Canadian history. He

had been Minister of Militia since 1911 and had caused considerable controversy during the initial stages of the war by replacing the army's orderly mobi-
lization plan with a "personal call to arms." Sir Sam can also be thanked for
scrapping the traditional regimental designations and substituting the num-
bered battalion system of the Canadian Expeditionary Force in the First World
War. His various exploits have caused even a sympathetic biographer to comment that he was *"persona non grata* with a considerable section of the people,
who looked upon him as a fanatical Orangeman . . . and a wind bag."[24] When he
was forced to resign from the Cabinet in 1916 after being barely cleared of cor-
ruption charges, an old rival called him "an embarrassment to the government"
and said, "no tears, no regrets, the nightmare is removed."[25]

Nevertheless, Sir Sam continued his interest in military and related matters. In May 1919 he said there was a mania in the country for building monuments. He had already been "asked to subscribe to fully three hundred monuments and other memorials in various parts of Canada." It may indicate the
rapid increase in monument building, or perhaps just something about Hughes,
but two days later the number of memorials he claimed he was being asked to
contribute to had risen to "a thousand and one." His solution was that a standard monument be mass-produced in various sizes and issued to communities
on the basis of their war losses. Many movements to erect monuments would
otherwise "end in muddles," Hughes argued, and people would waste millions.

Major-General S.C. Mewburn was the Minister of Militia to whom all these
questions, comments, and suggestions were ultimately directed. He was made
of different stuff than Sir Sam Hughes. After weighing the various proposals he
made his decision. He opted . . . to do nothing. Mewburn's inaction might have
been motivated by political or bureaucratic inertia, but his answer to Hughes,
dated on May 20, 1919, touches on some interesting issues:

> Such a system would give no play to the artistic feelings of the
> people. Standardization of objects of general use is no doubt a good
> thing as tending to cheapness of production; but it is not clear that
> standardization of objects of art and things beautiful or ornamental is
> a good thing. Do you not think also that people value things more
> highly if they have paid for them either in money or work or in some
> other way? My idea is that different locations should erect their own
> monuments and that if that involves some difficulty they will value
> them all the more on that account.

Following Mewburn's decision, all further inquiries were answered in the same
way. The government felt it advisable "to leave the matter to the discretion and
good judgement of the individual or corporation concerned." It suggested that
for each community "their own desires and taste should be consulted."

As a parting shot in the debate, Hughes predicted that the policy of government non-involvement would condemn memorials to being done in "a spasmodic sort of fashion."[26] Hughes' home town was Lindsay, Ontario. He had been a school teacher there and the editor and owner of the newspaper. A memorial with a handsome statue of a pensive soldier was completed in the town without government direction or financial assistance. There is only one other statue in the country that looks the same. Although Sir Sam did not die until 1921, his name is included among the fallen of the Great War that are engraved on that memorial.

The federal government would never have been able to finance memorials all over the country even if it had thought that the idea was a good one. The war debt it was carrying was enormous. Ottawa did, however, build some memorials of a national character. The huge double pylons on Vimy Ridge in France commemorate the most spectacular Canadian victory of the war and form the largest of several monuments that mark the battlefields of Europe. The carvings on the Vimy monument took Canadian sculptor Walter Allward several years to complete. The stone was specially quarried in Yugoslavia. Almost as well-known is George Clemeshaw's mourning soldier at St. Julien in Belgium, where Canadian troops suffered the first gas attack. The original tower on the Parliament Buildings in Ottawa had been destroyed in a fire in 1916, and when a new and taller one was built after the war it was dedicated as "The Peace Tower." The National Memorial in Ottawa's Confederation Square was built by the Department of Public Works. It features a group of bronze figures drawing a gun through a massive stone arch. The stone is from a quarry in Quebec and the sculptures were the work of the March family of Farnham, England. It was dedicated by King George VI during the royal tour in 1939.

The government also maintains the graves of veterans both in Canada and overseas through the Canadian branch of an international agency called the Commonwealth War Graves Commission. The Commission placed memorial crosses of standard design in some cemeteries including ones in Victoria, British Columbia, Regina, Saskatchewan, and Saint John, New Brunswick. As well, it built the Sailors' Memorial that stands at the entrance to Halifax Harbour, commemorating 3,249 men and 18 women lost at sea. Along with numerous historical plaques that mark old battlefields in Canada, that is the extent of Ottawa's involvement with memorials.

Almost as if to emphasize complete local autonomy with regard to memorials the army sent a bill for two dollars and ninety-five cents to the town of Petrolia, Ontario, in September 1922. This was to cover the train fare for the bugler, Private C. E. Ward, who had been sent from the garrison in London to play "The Last Post" and "Reveille" at the unveiling of the town's memorial.[27] When the citizens of Ganges, in the Gulf Islands of British Columbia, completed

Plaques on the Sailor's Memorial in Halifax's popular Point Pleasant Park list the names of men and women lost at sea during the wars. Street.

a permanent monument in 1923, they had to pay five dollars to let Private McVie and his instrument from the barracks in Victoria through a series of trains and ferry boats for the same purpose.[28] The army explained that these charges were made necessary "due to a paucity of funds."[29] Other support was equally hard to come by. In 1921 a Captain Henderson of the Bruce Militia in Walkerton, Ontario, had to write several memos before he was allowed to get a few rounds of blank ammunition for the firing of a salute at the dedication of the town's monument. The same year R. G. Eagles of Merritt, British Columbia, had to write to Victoria for permission to borrow a few rifles for the veterans' honour guard to carry at a memorial unveiling.

Even when units of the regular army itself wanted to erect memorials to fallen comrades they had to pay for them on their own. There are army memorials on government property at Royal Artillery Park in Halifax, at Vimy Barracks in Kingston, Ontario and on the base at Vedder Crossing, British Columbia, among other places. All were built by ex-servicemen. In the cold legal wording of an agreement to build a memorial at the barracks in London, Ontario, the Royal Canadian Regiment Old Comrades' Association agreed "to provide and pay for all material, labour, equipment, water, light, and power necessary for the preparation of the lands, the erection of the monument thereon and all work of construction related thereto."[30]

Rather than financially assisting in their construction the government actually found ways to use memorials to save money. The Department of Defence had been paying the City of Brantford two hundred and fifty dollars a year to maintain a piece of land beside the armouries. The decision to lease the property to the memorial committee was made in July 1931, on the condition that the committee take over the payments.[31]

The regular government bureaucrats were even parsimonious with moral support. Some veterans in Vernon, British Columbia, were asked to provide an honour guard for the dedication of the local monument. A certain Mr. Barber wrote to the army for advice, "as instructions contained in the Ceremonial Manual do not quite fit a ceremony of this nature."[32] He went on to say that "a few suggestions and a brief summary of the correct procedure would be very much appreciated as we are anxious to make a good showing." The most that such pleas ever got were rather sketchy do-it-yourself lessons. It is not known what exactly Mr. Barber and the Vernon veterans were told, but the answer to a similar request from the town of Alvinston, Ontario, said, "It is customary to cover the monument with a Union Jack, which is so held in place that it immediately drops when the cord is pulled."[33] That letter also thoughtfully included a few suggestions for appropriate hymns.

Examples of memorials being built by regional or local governments are also rare. A committee of the Ontario Legislature was appointed following the First World War "to consider how best to provide a permanent record" and "to report to the House in the next session."[34] In March 1921, after copious correspondence and numerous hearings a report was published by the King's Printer and duly tabled in the provincial legislature. It recommended, among other things, "a cenotaph or other form of monument at the head of University Avenue, Toronto, or some other suitable site in the city," and contained such phrases as, "a Memorial Hall of worthy proportions and architecture" to be "regarded as the Valhalla of the Province." It was not the first nor the last legislative report in Canadian history to be heard and promptly forgotten. There are a number of memorials at suitable sites in Toronto, but none of them was erected by the provincial government.

Municipal councils in Huron Township, Ontario, and Neepawa, Manitoba, committed tax revenue for the building of memorials. That, however, seems to have been a rare practice. The contribution of both local and provincial governments, when properties such as court houses were involved, was usually confined to to providing the land on which monuments were built. Of course, that could be a significant part of the cost. In Alvinston, the same Ontario town that received the scanty ceremonial instructions, the town gave the property on which the statue stands. In Pincher Creek, Alberta, the land was not donated and half of the two-thousand-dollar cost of the town's memorial went for the purchase of the site.

The C.P.R. was one of many companies to commemorate employees lost during World War I. This statue stands in Montreal's Windsor Station. Street.

Companies provided the initiative and financing for monuments about as infrequently as did governments. The Bowater Paper Company built a memorial for the town of Corner Brook, Newfoundland, but there were few other similar instances. Bowater also erected a commemorative stone in front of its plant for company employees who had been killed in the war. That was the kind of gesture made by most companies, and it was independent of whatever efforts were going on in the community as a whole. The Canadian Pacific Railway, for instance, had lost 1,115 workers in the course of the First World War. The company installed identical statues by Montreal artist Coeur de Lion MacCarthy at their stations in Montreal, Winnipeg, and Vancouver. The sculptures depict an angel bearing a fallen soldier from the battlefield. The CPR also put up plaques at many of their other facilities. The Bank of Montreal erected statues in their head office in Montreal and in front of their western headquarters near Portage and Main in Winnipeg. Massey-Harris built a stone column outside its farm implement works in Toronto. It not only includes the names of Canadian company employees lost in the war, but also workers at a number of foreign subsidiaries in the United States, France, the United Kingdom, and Australia.

Without the particular support or guidance of governments and generally, without the financial backing of either wealthy individuals, families or companies, movements intent on building memorials to lost soldiers sprang up spontaneously and simultaneously all over the country in the years after the First World War. They were most often started by some patriotic or veterans' group but came to include participants from the whole community. In the work these groups undertook, they often encountered difficulties, but the will to persist was there, judging from the number of monuments, from that era, that are to be seen today. A partial explanation for the kind of dedication that came to characterize memorial movements in the 1920s and 1930s can be found in the

Regina Leader of November 8, 1929. Reporting on the dedication of the cairn in Flaxcombe, Saskatchewan, the paper says, "The tenacity [sic] of purpose and 'esprit de corps' which carried the Canadian boys through the long eventful years of the Great War was never more exemplified than during the past year." A measure of the importance of monument building to towns and cities in Canada was expressed in the November 30 Peterborough *Examiner* in 1971: "The story behind the building of Peterborough's war memorial in Confederation Square is a story of community co-operation and achievement."

A figure representing Valour turns back barbarism on Walter Allward's dramatic monument created for Peterborough, Ontario. Street.

ERECTED AND DEDICATED
BY THE PEOPLE OF EUGENIA
AND COMMUNITY, TO THE
MEMORY OF HER SOLDIERS,
WHO FOUGHT AND DIED
IN THE GREAT WAR
1914 - 1918.

THREE
Did You Lose a Pal?

Quand ell'r'cevra cett' lettre
Tout ecrit' de sang,
Ses yeux baignant de larmes,
Son coeur sera mourant.
  "Chanson de Louis Riel"

Once memorial committees were formed, they quickly set about to build monuments on their own or quickly found out that they were on their own whether they liked it or not. Often their first task was to raise money. One of the few places where records of a memorial committee have been preserved is Curling, Newfoundland, an old community on the shores of a large inlet called the Bay of Islands in the western part of the province. Among the documents relating to the Bay of Islands memorial are copies of notices that appeared in newspapers as well as letters to specific groups and companies asking for donations. After describing the projected plan and its cost, one of these letters concludes, "The duty of raising this amount rests with the citizens and institutions of Humber District. We would request that you be generous to the fullest extent."[1] A somewhat more emotional appeal was made by the memorial committee in Stratford, Ontario:

> DID YOU LOSE A PAL IN THE WAR? Is there a man,
> woman or child in Stratford and its environs
> who does not number among the community's 300
> "soldier dead" at least one friend whose memory
> is precious and whose name and sacrifice they
> wish to perpetuate?
> CAN ANY MEMORIAL BE TOO COSTLY? Can any sacrifice
> of money be too great? They are lying beneath the
> poppies "out there" because they counted life

(opposite) The inscription on the base of this Ontario monument expresses a reality about the origin of memorials that was equally true in communities across the country. Street.

itself not too great a price to pay that the people
at home might never know the hell of Belgium and of
France, then surely IT IS A SACRED PRIVILEGE to
honour their deeds, their names, their sacrifice,
so next week give, as your heart dictates and your
purse permits, to Stratford's War Memorial.[2]

The prime movers in memorial drives were usually veterans' groups or patriotic women's organizations, but when it came to contributing to funds, virtually the whole population was involved in most places. Money was either donated directly or else collected through social events, tag days, sales, performances, and activities of various other kinds. One of the most poignant stories concerning the origin of a fund-raising effort was told to the 1927 meeting of the memorial committee in Edmonton. A member of the IODE explained that:

Boys play at the foot of the memorial obelisk in Curling, Newfoundland. It overlooks the beautiful fjord known as the Bay of Islands. Shipley.

Some time after the War began a man in the City of Edmonton was in need of some financial assistance which the Municipal Chapter of the Daughters of the Empire were able to give him. In his will he named the Municipal Chapter his beneficiaries and when he died overseas a sum of between $700.00 and $800.00 was given to the Chapter. They added enough to this to buy a Victory Bond and with the interest from this Bond gave a son and daughter of two soldiers who had given their lives in the War a business education here in the City. After it was found that there was no further pressing need for this money to be used for educational purposes the Chapter passed a resolution that the original fund should form the nucleus of a War Memorial Fund for Edmonton.[3]

In some instances donations swelled funds fairly quickly and easily. The Veterans' Association in Battleford, Saskatchewan, collected eight hundred dollars in a single door-to-door canvass of their town that lasted only three hours. The minutes of the memorial committee in Red Deer, Alberta, show us how they divided the city and district into fifteen areas, with a canvass captain appointed in each. The resolution that had been passed at the first public meeting

One of the most ornate memorials in Canada is Soldier's Tower at Hart House, University of Toronto. In spite of its expense there was no trouble raising the funds to build it. The same was not true elsewhere. Street.

concerning the memorial was printed on the back of a card and the front was left for the amount that people were willing to subscribe. The canvassers, mostly women, carried these cards on Wednesday, October 6, 1921, when they visited everyone in Red Deer. Most of the five thousand dollars needed for the monument was pledged that day. The University of Toronto Soldiers' Memorial Fund was so over-subscribed that even after the enormous expenditure of one hundred and seventy five thousand dollars the building of the Gothic revival tower that commemorates the six hundred and twenty former students killed in the First World War, there was a surplus. The extra was used to establish a loan fund.

Lists of contributors and amounts given were often printed in the newspapers. (This had also been a fairly common practice during the fund-raising for memorials following the Boer War.) Such lists from 1919 in Goderich, Ontario, and 1925 in North Battleford, Saskatchewan, include not only the names of old established families in those communities. Names such as Judge Dickson, Reverend Munroe, Mr. and Mrs. Blythe, and Dr. Field were joined by donors such as Mr. Coppock of North Battleford, and Mon Lay, of the West Street Laundry in Goderich.

Groups contributed as well. Even organizations that were not usually associated with one another or were traditionally antagonistic joined their efforts for the sake of memorials to the fallen. The newspaper in Goderich, Ontario, acknowledged a contribution of eighty-nine dollars and eighty cents from the Catholic Holy Name Society. The money had been raised at a euchre party. It is a safe bet that not a cent of the twenty-five dollars from the Victoria Street Methodist Church came from card playing. On a list of contributors from Deer Lake, Newfoundland, in 1930, we find both the Archbishop Howley Council of the Knights of Columbus and the Star of the West Lodge of the True Blue and Loyal Orange Order, indicating a unity of purpose not always achieved easily in this country.

In Stratford, Ontario, public servants, companies, and workers are all shown as contributors to the memorial fund. Fire Chief Kappele sent a cheque for twenty-five dollars from the Fire Brigade. The Whyte Pork Packing Company contributed five hundred dollars and the Irving Umbrella Company, manufacturers of Broadway, Peerless and Perfection brand parasols and sunshades, put in fifteen dollars. Thirty-two employees of the George McLegan Furniture Company collected eighty-five dollars and fifty cents among them. The names of all the employees are listed except for the person who could only afford the fifty cents. This was similar to the lists in the newspaper where many modest donors were listed as A Friend, A Citizen, or Anonymous. Boards of Trade, the Elks' Lodge, the Bank of Montreal, Smith's Art Store, the Glenrose Homemakers, the Knitting Mill Employees, the Knights of Pythias, and every other institution, business, and denomination added to the memorial funds.

It seems natural enough that local projects such as memorials would derive most of their support from the immediate vicinity. The extent to which funding was limited to the particular locality, however, helps to underscore the parochial nature of movements to build monuments. One contributor to the Goderich, Ontario, fund was from New York – a native of Goderich who had moved away some years before the war. Judging from the number of times the paper mentioned this distant though modest donation, outside help must have been a novelty. The correspondence from Curling, Newfoundland, records not only those who did contribute, but also those who declined. The rule seems to have been that local groups, companies, bank branches, and so on responded positively while those further away did not feel inclined to give even if they had an interest in the area. Such groups and companies were no doubt contributing to memorial funds in their own localities. The central office of the Newfoundland Veterans' Association did not give money to the Curling monument, although they were asked, and a Halifax-based shipping company that did business in the Bay of Islands region also declined. In Barrie, Ontario, the plan had been to erect one monument for the town and the surrounding rural townships, but the more distant of the outlying mu-

The money to pay for this handsome memorial statue in Red Deer, Alberta was pledged in a single day. Shipley.

nicipalities eventually opted to withdraw and build its own memorial. After a meeting with representatives of the United Farmers of Alberta, the chairman of the memorial committee in Red Deer, Alberta, reported to his colleagues that "from the impression received at that meeting, he felt that those in the immediate vicinity of the city would give their support, but those in outlying districts" could not be depended on for much support as they were undertaking memorials of their own.[4]

If the contributions to funds testify to the popular interest in memorials, the ways in which they were collected indicate the ingenuity of memorial committees. When it came to raising money through community activities a good deal of enthusiasm was generated by events that were often intended to be enjoyable. Older residents of the London, Ontario, suburb of Manor Park remember the memorial fund concerts given by Jolly's Band in the old orchard. They also recall devious neighbourhood boys who dropped green apples from the overhanging trees down the tubas. Theatre benefits are mentioned among the funding sources in both North Battleford, Saskatchewan, and Goderich, Ontario. Teas, fetes, and dances also became popular. The memorial committee ladies' auxiliary of Chester, Nova Scotia, hosted a garden party. One can picture the ladies dressed in 1920s fashions standing outside one of the town's crisply painted, white, weatherboard houses. The event raised fourteen hundred dollars towards the cost of shipping the memorial statue from New York, where it was being cast by a summer visitor to Chester, J. Massey Rhind. At the far end of the country, in 1923, bright uniforms and beautiful gowns were the order of the day at the Memorial Fund Ball in Victoria, British Columbia. The November 11, 1923 edition of the *Daily Colonist* said that "it was by common consent, a worthy observance of a great anniversary," and went on to talk of the "desire to make Armistice Day, by fitting symbol and by simple ceremony, a day in the calendar commensurate with its meaning in the lives of succeeding men."

Some fairly novel fund-raising schemes were tried. Dr. Norman Craig was the physician for forty-three years in the Ontario town of Fergus. The good doctor was also something of a dramatist. He had served as a pilot in the Great War and wrote a play about his wartime experience called *You're Lucky If You're Killed.* The proceeds from the performance of the play went towards building the town's memorial. (Dr. Craig must have been well thought of by the people he served because they later built a memorial to him as well.) St. John's, Newfoundland, saw one of the most original fund-raising ventures of all in 1922. Thousands of leaflets were dropped over the city from one of those new inventions, an airplane. The leaflets were printed on one side:

Souvenir
of
First Memorial Flight
over
St. John's and Vicinity
In connection with
Newfoundland War Memorial Campaign[5]

On the reverse side, finders were told that by returning the leaflet to a certain address along with a donation, they would be eligible for a draw, with the winner getting the "much coveted chance for a flight in the Aeroplane."

The amounts of money collected in these various ways were quite sizable. The monument that stands at the top of a hill on the main street in Sherbrooke, Quebec, with its three bronze soldiers and winged angel, all cast in Brussels, cost twenty-five thousand dollars. The carillon bells for Norfolk County's Memorial Tower in Simcoe, Ontario, were brought from England, and the monument represents an expenditure of thirty-thousand dollars. Camrose, Alberta, spent sixty-five hundred dollars on a monument. Elgin, Manitoba, spent thirty four hundred dollars and Lunenburg, Nova Scotia, four thousand dollars on statues. In smaller communities the amounts may have been less but the per capita cost of a memorial was often more. Between the census of 1911 and 1921 the population of rural communities in Canada remained fairly constant or declined, reflecting the large-scale movement of people from country to city. In these smaller centres, during the time that monuments were being built the expenditure for memorials often exceeded a dollar per person. The memorial statue in Harriston, Ontario, cost sixty-three hundred dollars, while the population of the town in 1911 was only 4,165. In the southern Ontario township of West Nissouri a population of 2,428 paid for a memorial that cost three thousand dollars. That meant one dollar and fifty-two cents and one dollar and twenty-three cents respectively for every man, woman, and child in these communities. Children are included here not simply for statistical neatness but because collecting money for memorials was something they were very much involved with. Many people still remember the nickel donations they made as schoolchildren. Although from an earlier era, the Boer War monument in Ottawa actually recognizes the contributions of children in its inscription.

At the present time a nickel or even a dollar does not sound like very much. Neither do totals like six thousand dollars or even thirty thousand dollars seem impressive when compared to much larger sums that are common for projects of any kind today. But these amounts did represent much more at the time memorials were built. An illustration of inflation with regard to a monument can be seen in Edmonton. During the years after 1967 a proposal was debated in that city about moving the city's memorial. The first estimates for the move were in the neighbourhood of twenty thousand dollars. By 1973 the monument had still not budged an inch and the figure for the move was up to seventy thousand dollars. When the job was finally done in 1978 the price tag was one hundred and thirty thousand dollars. That was thirteen times the original ten thousand dollars cost of the monument when it was erected in 1936. The initial cost had included not only buying and carving the granite, but also transporting it hundreds of kilometres from Vancouver Island. The 1978 move covered only a few blocks in downtown Edmonton.

Many of Canada's community war memorials are like this one in Trochu, Alberta – very modest. Shipley.

If monuments were not built and paid for by the time of the Great Depression, their promoters often had a very difficult time. Some of the last documents from the Curling, Newfoundland, collection record the fact that even after the memorial was completed there were still a couple of hundred dollars worth of outstanding bills. Before the Veterans' Association consented to make up the difference, a detailed accounting of all expenditures was demanded and received. The monument in Brantford, Ontario, was not dedicated until 1933. It consists of a very imposing shaft of stone on an extensive base with steps leading up to it. The original plans, however, called for an even more impressive work complete with statues. The sculpted figures were never completed. A statue that was planned for a memorial in Belleville, Ontario, also never materialized.

The average income in the 1920s was about eighteen hundred dollars a year for an office worker or supervisor. It was perhaps one thousand dollars a year for a factory worker.[6] It is true that things also cost much less than now. In 1925, a chicken dinner could be had at the Brown Betty Tea Room on King Street in Toronto for 60 cents. Coffee was 59 cents a pound, cheese 22 cents a pound. At Fairweather's Men's Shop you paid ten dollars and fifty cents for a raincoat and you could buy a Ford truck at Riverdale Garage on the Danforth for two hundred twenty-five dollars. By the 1930s not too much had changed – if you still had a job. The trouble was thousands of people didn't. The raincoat was a bargain for nine dollars and eighty cents in 1932 but that was at Robinson's going-out-of-business sale. Bacon was still 17 cents a pound, but cheese was half its 1925 price and coffee was down to 29 cents.[7]

All of that meant two things in terms of monuments. One was that the dollar went much further when it came to paying for workmanship and materials. The best of these things cost relatively less than they do today. It was possible to obtain the finest marble, granite, and original cast bronze statues if you could raise the money. Carving a stone statue might take a skilled craftsman six to eight months, but at the Thompson Monument Company in Toronto he was paid only fifty cents an hour. The other side of this was that a dollar per person meant a much greater financial commitment in the depression years. A fairly well-off wage-earner may have been making between one and two thousand dollars a year, but if the family consisted of five people, then its proportional contribution to a memorial effort would have been five dollars. A worker in a similar situation today would be earning between fifteen and twenty-five thousand dollars a year, and the donation, if it represented an equal portion of the family income, would be fifty or sixty dollars.

One surviving memorial subscription list from the time is from Lark Harbour, Newfoundland. The money was collected by Leonard Purdy, the lighthouse keeper at Little Port. The largest single sum given by any of the seventy-one people on the list was three dollars. Most could only manage contributions

of twenty-five, thirty or fifty cents. As is the case today, the fishermen of the
East Coast were not earning anything like the incomes of office or factory workers in central Canada. Cod, their main product, was fetching less than two cents
a pound on the international market in 1932.[8] People in other resource and
primary industries such as farming were not well paid either. And the rural
population still made up half of the total number of people in the country.
When we think of the countless contributions of a dollar here and a few cents
there that were needed to finance memorials the effort appears incredible.
When we think that the money came from people who fished from open boats
in the icy Atlantic, plowed the dusty fields of the prairies with horses, or toiled
in factories without the benefits of worker's compensation, unemployment insurance, or the eight-hour day, the investment in memorials is even more
remarkable.[9] The inscriptions on memorials in New Harbour, Newfoundland,
and New Westminster, British Columbia, begin: "Erected by the people." The
plaque on a memorial in rural Ontario reads: "This monument was erected by
the Ladies' Patriotic League of Waverly and Voluntary Public Subscription."
"By the people" or "by public subscription" could legitimately be carved on the
majority of monuments found in Canada.

*Whether the story that this statue in Oxford, Nova Scotia was erected backwards, facing away
from the street is true or not, extra funds for something like moving a monument were seldom
available. Street.*

Collecting money was not always the road that memorial committees took to reach their goal. Partly from the lack of potential funds, but more for the sincerity of the gesture, some groups decided to build monuments themselves, with volunteer labour and contributed materials. In these places financial outlay was minimal while people's feelings were demonstrated directly through hard work.

On the shores of Lake Huron, in the village of Bayfield, Ontario, an ex-soldier named Rev. F. H. Paul was the guiding spirit in the building of the memorial. It was 1933 when he and three other veterans began gathering suitable granite stones from the bed of the Bayfield River. What they had in mind was the building of a cairn. Soon others joined them, and by July of that year they had enough fieldstone to construct a pyramid that was twenty feet high. Far away from the Great Lakes, another fishing port on the Atlantic coast also owed part of its memorial to volunteer labour. With teams of draught horses several farmers in the vicinity of Chester, Nova Scotia, hauled a huge boulder some six miles to the site of the memorial. A local stone worker, Wakefield Zinck, fashioned a unique pedestal for a statue out of this single rock. A similar story unfolded in 1937 on Bowen Island near Vancouver. William Linklater built the forms for the concrete, and J. Collins and some other men from the Legion helped with mixing and pouring and eventually covering the monument with stucco.

At times this type of project developed into something that involved quite large numbers of people. In 1923 the citizens of Moossomin, Saskatchewan, levelled the site for their memorial statue. The Regina *Leader* of May 7, 1928 reported that at least a hundred local farmers, along with a number of men and boys from the town, gathered for the work. It was estimated that eight hundred loads of earth were moved. The Victoria *Daily Colonist* carried a story on November 11, 1923 of what happened in the Vancouver Island community of Courtenay in 1921, when "a host of owners of wagons and motor trucks" showed up to help with construction of the memorial in the town.

For some localities the concept of contributed labour took on a special meaning. The schoolchildren in the Ontario village of Vienna each brought to class a stone as large as they could carry. From these individual tributes, with special meaning for each child, a cairn was erected in front of the school. In Tisdale, Saskatchewan, it was the families of men killed in the war who collected fieldstones for the monument. The careful gathering of stones from the very countryside where the fallen men had lived and worked was important to those who built memorials. The sea cliffs around Charlos Cove, Nova Scotia, are very steep. They are too steep in fact to make it possible to carry large quantities of beach shingle up to the top. The cairn in front of the Legion Hall in Charlos Cove was therefore made from stone that was brought from Larry's River, several kilometres down the road. There are people in Charlos Cove, however, who

The placement of this beautiful monument in Guelph, Ontario was the subject of a civic plebicite. Shipley.

still insist that the stones from their own beach would have looked better. When Miss Holliday spoke to a meeting in Guelph, Ontario, in 1921, she "hoped that all or part of the monument could be erected from Guelph stone, thus weaving into the monument a little bit of what the men fought for."[10]

Businesses and governments, though seldom solely responsible for building memorials, often contributed goods and services in a way similar to the contribution of labour from individuals. The plot of land in Pembroke, Ontario, where the town's memorial statue stands, was donated by one of the leading local families. The memorial site in Broadview, Saskatchewan, was supplied by the local council. Material for the monument in Point Edward, Ontario, was contributed by the Central Canada Stone Company. There were several requests from the Bay of Islands Memorial Committee in Curling, Newfoundland, for donations of goods and services from companies and government departments. Free shipment of the memorial stone itself, to come from Scotland, was arranged on the return voyage of one of the International Power and Paper Company's steamers as the company's pulp and paper mill in Corner Brook was the major industry in the area. The Highroads Commission was what the Newfoundland roads department was called in those days. It allowed the memorial committee to take some gravel from one of its quarries to be used in constructing the base for the monument. The Highroads Commission was duly thanked by the committee secretary, who wrote: "I give you assurance of taking only what may be required for the work." The secretary went on to say that "already offers have been made by teamsters for its free transportation from the quarry to the Court House Hill, Curling." The old Court House had been donated by the Newfoundland government as a site for the monument, but the committee was able to sell the building itself for demolition. The one hundred and twenty-five dollars they received was added to the fund. When the pieces of the memorial arrived, a Newfoundland Railway spokesman wrote: "If you require the crane to unload War Memorial material at Curling, permission will be granted for you to move same over the Railway on the understanding, of course, that the time will be arranged with Superintendent Cobb so that it will not interfere with train movements."[11]

Whatever ease or difficulty memorial committees faced in collecting money or arranging the contributions of the material and labour needed to complete monuments, it seems to have been a gratifying experience for most communities. After the ball games had been played and the ladies of Cookstown, Ontario, had served a fine lunch at the memorial picnic, it is reported that one of the committee members whose name was Monkman spoke to the assembled villagers. It is hard to mistake the warmth that Mr. Monkman was feeling when he said, as quoted in the Barrie *Northern Advance*, June 7, 1917, that the committee wanted to "express their unbounded thankfulness for and appreciation of the wholehearted response to the call to assist in the undertaking which is marked by success beyond all expectation."

The central location given to war memorials in many Canadian communities reflects the symbolic importance afforded them. Shipley.

FOUR
The Constant Clamour

I am the
passionate Statue
in each of your parks
I am the
poet in his pure
air
(remember and
       beware)
Don Gutteridge: "Tecumseh: Dreams and Vision"

By their nature public monuments are community property. People had to sense a degree of personal participation in the creation of a monument in order to accept it as the focus of such an important ceremony as Remembrance Day. To have been maintained and to continue to have a measure of significance for a population, monuments had to reflect some collective feeling. The organizations that began and sustained efforts to erect memorials in Canadian towns and cities were local and broadly representative. Similarly, the voluntary contributions of labour and money came from all parts of the community. But people did not simply want to be involved in committees, work gangs, and canvassing teams. That only partially satisfied their need for community expression.

Even more important than local initiative in the area of organization and funding, the decisions on form, design, and location of memorials had to be an agreeable distillation of the popular will. In the diverse and sometimes factious communities that make up the Canadian patchwork, legitimate consensus often demanded lengthy and animated debate. In these discussions individuals and groups had either to express their desires or at least to feel that their views were represented. Without that participation and acceptance, monuments would

(opposite) Long before bilingual signs were required by regulation the insciptions on memorials such as this one in St. Lambert, Quebec were written in both English and French. Street.

never have been built or else would have disappeared the first time an administration changed or a street needed widening.

Communities usually began their memorial projects with the gathering of information. J. Holman was the president of the memorial committee in Summerside, Prince Edward Island. Long before the life-sized bronze statue of a charging soldier was erected in Summerside's public park, he was sending letters all over the country addressed to other memorial committees. Under the elaborate letterhead that pictured Holman's Catalogue Department Store, recipients were asked what sorts of memorials were planned in their areas. Similar requests for ideas came to various memorial committees from the Brantford, Ontario, Chamber of Commerce and from the editor of the Ottawa *Evening Journal* on behalf of those who wanted to build a monument in the capital. The committee in Oshawa, Ontario, boasted that it had written all over the world. The people in Flaxcombe, Saskatchewan, were not as grandiose in their claims as their eastern cousins, but they were more direct in their method. Their committee travelled throughout the province of Saskatchewan to see what others were doing.

The Oshawa, Ontario memorial committee wrote all over the world for ideas of how to commemorate their war losses. The monument they built includes pieces of stone from some of the places they wrote as well as some of the World War I battlefields. Street.

In 1927 Mayor A.U.G. Bury of Edmonton sent a rather formally worded letter to sixteen fellow mayors in towns and cities from Halifax to Vancouver. His request, if not his diction, was fairly typical:

> A movement is now on foot in this city to erect some form of memorial to the soldiers who fell in the Great War; and as chairman of the committee having the matter in charge I am desirous of gathering preliminary information upon the following points:
>
> 1. The better form – cenotaph or monument (i.e. pedestal with figure or figures).
> 2. The best kind of site; on a street in the centre of the city where the tide of business life would flow by it in the fullest and most constant volume; or in some park space.
> 3. The relative costliness of cenotaph on the one hand and a monument on the other. If your City either already has erected or is proposing to erect such a memorial may I ask you to favour me with the finding of your authorities on these points.[1]

From his wording of the question concerning location it is clear that Mayor Bury had his own strong views on the subject. But then almost everyone did.

Once people began to have notions of the possibilities for memorials, lively discussions blossomed on the editorial pages of local papers. From editorials and letters to the editor the debate spilled over into council chambers, club meetings, and even open gatherings called to discuss the choices. Various views were expressed and circulated for public consideration. Promoters of different memorial concepts enlisted adherents and waged campaigns to convince others that their ideas were suitable. A few voices even spoke against having any sort of monument at all. On July 17, 1925 the radical Halifax *Citizen* called plans for a city memorial a "war glorifying scheme." Such opposition was rare but the polemical language used was not. All the typical journalistic and rhetorical techniques were called upon. In 1919 the *Reporter* in Gananoque, Ontario, said that "council's chambers rang with debate on the issue for the next year."[2]

The first and most important choice was whether a community should have a purely symbolic memorial or something practical. Symbolic memorials could take the form of either a monument or a cenotaph. By "monument" people usually meant a statue or group of figures on a pedestal, while the term "cenotaph" generally referred to a plain stone shaft. Edmonton's Mayor Bury made this distinction in his letter to other cities. Practical or living memorials, on the other hand, were hospitals, parks, schools, concert halls, or any other structure that would be dedicated to the memory of the community's dead while at the same time serving some ongoing function.

Practicality was and is a deeply rooted Canadian value. Survival in the northern wilderness had spawned a people known more for their functional approach to problems than for their aesthetic interests, and bush-sense lingered on. Northrop Frye calls it the garrison mentality – the consequence of living in a small protected space separated from the hostile environment by a flimsy wall – and he talks about Susanna Moodie's "constant fight to be clean, fully clothed," and "disciplined in speech."[3] There was not too much room in the Canadian psyche for frills. At the extreme was the suggestion made by the Halifax *Citizen* on December 16, 1926: "Use the fifty thousand, if it is available, as the nucleus of a fund for erecting modern tenements in Halifax which is one of the greatest needs for the city." A compromise was found in the appeal of the "living memorial," something useful, and the attraction was very strong indeed. A November 11, 1920 letter to the editor of the *Tillsonburg News* in Tillsonburg, Ontario, stated flatly that most people were in favour of a memorial park where one could go for a quiet walk with friends. The writer added that the park could also be used for sporting events. In 1921 the December 12 *Northern Advance* in Barrie, Ontario, carried a letter from the Reverend Dean O'Malley: "I would propose something useful to the soldiers themselves. Anything in brass or bronze is all right in the Old Country where there are more people to admire them." The suggestion had been made that a memorial YMCA be built, and an editorial in the December 19 paper argued that "the YMCA has done so much for the boys at the front that the establishment of such an institution in Barrie would certainly be a fitting way to commemorate the war. It would be a temporary home for young fellows from various parts of the county who visited Barrie, and members of the YMCA at Orillia and other places would have the full use of it while in town." It is clear that the editor was thinking not just of a memorial but of his town's position as the main centre in the area. When someone else proposed a memorial hospital for Barrie, the supporters of the YMCA idea again appealed to the principle of practicality by claiming that a Y would keep young men healthy and out of hospital.[4]

On November 10, 1922 the *Vancouver Sun* ran an editorial that supported a memorial idea that would have doubled as a city-works project. The west-coaster's statements should amuse good-natured prairie dwellers:

No finer memorial could be erected to the sons of BC who gave their lives overseas than an avenue of beautiful green trees, each bearing a brass plaque inscribed with the name of a dead soldier.

This type of memorial has been adopted in several Australian cities, in some American cities, and even in treeless, sand-swept Saskatoon.

In this latter city where energetic men are carving a place of beauty out of a bald windy patch of prairie, the avenue of memorial trees will have to be carefully nursed along to maturity.

The paper went on to say that it would be much easier to grow the memorial trees in British Columbia.

The proponents of functional memorials often seemed to feel that the value of their ideas was self-evident. J. W. D. Turner was a veteran of the First World War and was serving as sergeant-at-arms in the Alberta legislature when he wrote to Ottawa in 1918. He submitted a picture of a monument designed by his son. In a reply from a federal official, Turner was told that the government had already taken steps to provide an "important, massive memorial at Ottawa," and that "such a memorial would doubtless take the form of a building."[5]

A number of these so-called living memorials were erected. There is Soldiers' Memorial Hospital in Middleton, Nova Scotia, and other memorial hospitals in Twillingate, Newfoundland, and in Orillia, St. Thomas, and Perth, Ontario. There are memorial halls in Carman, Manitoba, and Aggassiz, British Columbia. There are arenas like the one in Smiths Falls, Ontario, and numerous memorial libraries across the country. But in spite of the great appeal of the practical memorial, the overwhelming evidence in the parks and on the main streets of Canadian cities points to the fact that more often than not people opted in the last analysis for the symbolic. Even in those places where buildings of some kind were constructed, a monument was often erected outside them sooner or later. A statue of a soldier stands in front of the Memorial Hospital in St. Thomas, Ontario, and an inscribed stone stands beside the Memorial Arena in Smith's Falls.

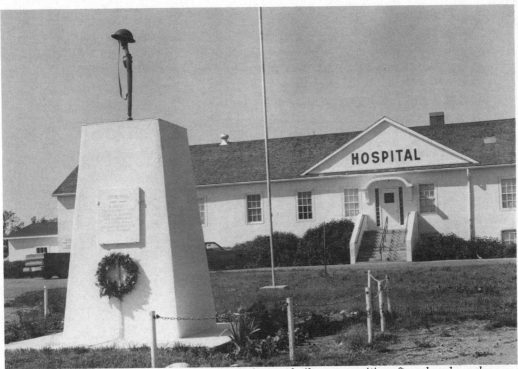

Even when practical memorials such as hospitals were built, communities often placed purely symbolic memorials as well. That was the case in Delisle, Saskatchewan. Shipley.

People did not write or talk much about why they felt the need to erect monuments instead of or in addition to memorial structures. Once various options were discussed the decisions were, for the most part, tacit. Many papers that had carried stories on the debates ended their coverage as did the August 11, 1928 issue of the Oshawa *Daily Times:* "A public meeting was called and the general outline of the memorial was adopted without one dissenting vote, without one word of adverse criticism." Oshawa erected a statue. The record of the memorial movement in Brantford, Ontario, is equally brief about the decision that was made: "As a result of initial conferences it was decided that the tribute should take the form of a monument."[6] In Gananoque, Ontario, "increasing pressure from citizen groups and the constant clamour for a monument decided council in favour of the project."[7]

The same Edmonton mayor who wrote letters all over the country asking for opinions on memorial options also placed advertisements in the city's newspapers inviting comment from citizens. He also solicited suggestions from the city's service clubs. There were many replies to the mayor's appeal:

> . . . I have been requested by the Executive to advise you of the following resolution, approved by the Kiwanis Public Affairs Committee and the Club . . .
> . . . In reply to your request made to the Gyro Club on Tuesday 27th ultimo for an expression of opinion on the above, the matter was duly considered and the following resolution unanimously accepted . . .
> . . . seeing by your letter that you invited public opinions in regard to the proposed cenotaph . . .
> . . . replying to your request for the opinion of the Optimist Club on the question of a Cenotaph, I quote from the minutes of the Executive Committee . . . [8]

Almost without exception the answer to the mayor's question was this: a monument to be paid for by public subscription should be built.

Hints of people's reasons for choosing monuments do survive in some written records. In Newfoundland, July 1 rather than November 11 is the main day designated for remembering the war dead. It is the anniversary of the 1916 Battle of Beaumont Hamel, where the Newfoundland Regiment was decimated. After the Remembrance Day observance in St. John's, in 1919, the *Daily News* carried this editorial: "Whatever views may be held concerning the memorial to be erected to our fallen heroes, yesterday's function removed all doubts as to the wisdom of erecting a monument around which year after year the people of the town can gather and pay respect to the memory of our noble dead."[9]

As well as wanting a memorial that had a special and unique commemorative function, people were also concerned about permanence. Often the suggestion was made that a plaque or dedication in the entrance to a practical building serve as a memorial. Barrie, Ontario, was one of the many places where this solution was proposed. But Dr. Sprott raised an objection: "If we put this tablet in a building it may not be here 100 years from now. I think a statue would be more lasting."[10] A memorial committee member in Winnipeg was reported in *The Free Press*, June 14, 1920 to have spoken at one point about a monument of "imperishable granite." Fears about the impermanence of buildings turned out to be well justified since many structures built as memorials in the 1920s and 1930s have become outdated, redundant, and some have even been abandoned and torn down. As for the feelings of the returned veterans themselves, the story of the monument in Barrie again provides some insight: "Mr. Kendall, secretary of the GWVA had a petition circulated amongst the returned men so as to be sure of their real opinion as to what kind of memorial they wished. They favour a monument placed in a conspicuous [sic] place. 'The men,' said he, 'want nothing but an unselfish memorial, something symbolic. The men would be bitterly opposed to anything for themselves.'"[11] The sentiment was the same in Chatham, Ontario: "The views of the returned men were ascertained, likewise those of men employed in factories. Twenty-four hundred and twenty-two of the aggregate pronounced themselves as being heartily in favour of a monument and the site chosen."[12]

Once the decision to build a monument had been taken, committees invited sculptors, architects, and stonecutters to submit designs and estimates. Competition among the individuals and firms interested and capable of producing monuments was stiff. There were twenty-two designs submitted for the competition in Welland, Ontario, ten by sculptors and twelve by architects. In Lachute, Quebec, there were thirty proposals. And even in the smaller centres there were seldom fewer than three entries. The memorial committee minutes from March 3, 1921, in Red Deer, Alberta, tell us what happened when designs were considered there:

> The chairman explained that the meeting had been called to consider plans, designs, location etc. and that a report should be made at this meeting to submit to a public meeting to be called later. There were three Monumental Firms who had representatives present and would submit their designs, and give us any information we desired. Mr. R. L. Gaetz suggested that we ask each representative to submit their designs etc. individually and that the chairman request the representatives to retire from the meeting in order that the members may discuss each design.[13]

Three Toronto-based firms, the Thompson Monument Works, McIntosh Granite Company, and Canadian William A. Rogers Limited, Foundry Department (later F. G. Tickell and Sons) were the most active bidders for memorials. Handsome catalogues showing arsenals of statuary still exist for at least two of the companies.[14] The foreword to the Rogers catalogue reads: "We present to you these few illustrations so that you may obtain an idea of the Memorial Tablets and Honour Rolls that other Townships, Schools, Churches etc. have erected. On request we will send you illustrations of many other designs and sizes. We are prepared to furnish you with a full-sized sketch of any design or combination of designs that may be selected, and this without placing you under any obligation." On the cover was the title "Art Bronze" and a picture of an an angel sculpture called "The Herald of Peace." The McIntosh booklet was more frankly entitled "War Memorials." It contained pictures of the Boer War statues the company had erected in Toronto and London, Ontario. Its approach was also more direct. "When you decide to erect a public or private soldiers' memorial . . . questions as to design, location, material, cost and contractor at once arise." The problem of permanence was recognized by McIntosh as well. "For the larger memorials in the open air, granite and bronze are, in this climate, the only satisfactory material." The McIntosh Granite Company spoke of its thirty-five years' experience in erecting memorials and did not shy away from mention of expense. "Special designs to meet conditions of location or cost or embody your own ideas, prepared without charge. Where a definite sum is available for the work, we submit designs obtainable for that price."

Business was good. Frank Tickell began as a salesman for the Rogers Company but within a couple of years after the war he was in partnership with his father and brother in a firm of their own. The price of growth was a certain amount of bad feeling between contractor and prospective client, left in the wake of the hard sell. There was definite agitation in the tone of a letter from Lieutenant Colonel F. B. Ware, a military official in London, Ontario, declining an offer from Tickell to provide designs and prices. The letter of solicitation the colonel was answering in October 1923 was not the first sent by the energetic Tickells.[15] Their efforts did pay off in many places, however. They supplied statues to the Ontario communities of Sarnia, Shelbourne, Streetsville, Rannock, and St. Marys, to name just a few. Tickell figures are also found as far away from the firm's Toronto foundry as Wolfville, Nova Scotia.

Certain artists had their devotees. One can understand the enthusiasm of a certain Mr. Taylor, an insurance executive from Winnipeg. He wrote several times to Edmonton, and probably other places, encouraging the committees to commission statues by the same sculptor who had completed the memorial in Prince Albert, Saskatchewan – none other than Mr. Taylor's wife, Hilliard Taylor. Prince Albert's monument depicts the spirit of Canada in the form of a woman holding a laurel wreath over the grain elevators in the town below. It was said to be the first instance of the nation represented by a symbolic figure. It is less clear why the mayor of Halifax spent so much energy pushing the work

Not many monument competitions had the elaborate submissions pictured here during judging for the National War Memorial in Ottawa but many artists, architects and builders vied for each commission. PAC.

of New York sculptor J. Massey Rhind. Rhind had done the figure on the cenotaph in Halifax and perhaps the mayor felt some civic prestige was to be had from other cities following his city's lead.[16]

In Curling, Newfoundland, letters offering "to furnish you with designs and prices" arrived from marble and granite companies in Nova Scotia and St. John's even before the committee had had time to request them. The St. John's firm, Muir and Company, began its sales pitch by describing how inferior Nova Scotia granite was compared to its own product.[17] St. Stephen, New Brunswick, was the scene of another case of a hard sell by the traditional monument dealers, who tried to get a representative on the memorial committee. They then donated money to the cause. Finally, their man gave a moving speech about "our boys" just as he produced a contract, ready to sign, from his pocket. While memorial committees often fell for this, in St. Stephen the plan was foiled by Frances Loring, an energetic artist who lived in Toronto. She showed up in the town with a model of the statue she was offering. The committee members postponed their decision, and when they made up their minds they chose Loring's mourning soldier figure.[18]

In spite of sales pressure and the diverse views that existed in Canada's heterogeneous communities, the choices of designs and locations of monuments generally represented a popular consensus. St. Stephen was not taken in by the monument companies, and Curling, Newfoundland, chose neither of the firms that petitioned its committee without invitation. The sculptures of Hilliard Taylor and Massey Rhind had to line up and be judged with other submissions. Of the three designs presented to the committee in Chatham, Ontario, neither the most nor the least expensive was selected. The handsome statues in the McIntosh and Tickell catalogues had to compete with numerous others. In each case it was the desire of the people in the specific locality that prevailed. After the Red Deer, Alberta, memorial committee had decided at an open meeting to place its statue in the centre of the street in front of the post office, the city engineer suggested another spot that would be easier from his point of view. The committee answered that the site was the will of the people and the engineer would just have to accommodate it.[19]

North Portal, Saskatchewan, was small enough that when the time came to make some final choices concerning the memorial everyone who had donated to the fund was given a vote. In Guelph, Ontario, the choices among three potential locations were put on the ballot during the municipal election of 1921. In larger places, and where more complicated decisions made direct voting impracticable, advisory groups made up of citizens with particular expertise assessed the possibilities. They weighed the competing designs against what the community wanted and picked the most suitable one. Such an advisory board chose the memorial for Welland, Ontario. In its report the board explained the decision:

In judging this competition the jury gave serious consideration to the following points:

1. The suitability of the memorial to the site, having regard to the shape and size of the plot, the character of the surrounding landscape and the visibility of the monument, both from the land side and from the canal. There is a very large travel movement by boat and it was considered by the jury that any monument that was erected should be visible and intelligible to the passengers on the slow-moving boats.
2. That the monument should, by its form or by definite symbolism, clearly indicate its character, this entirely aside from any written inscription on the monument itself. Or to put it another way, that it should tell the story and indicate its Canadian ancestry.
3. That the monument should be of sufficient size and scale (within the given cost range) that in mass it would not be insignificant.
4. That in general composition as well as in detail, it should have distinction, balance, beauty of form and line.[20]

Winnipeg sculptress Hilliard Taylor created this allegorical figure of Canada for the monument in Prince Albert, Saskatchewan. Shipley.

The monument in Welland has a soldier in a Canadian uniform protecting a woman who is carrying a sheaf of wheat. The statue was finally located away from the canal and was put in a park along with the extraordinary rose garden that gives Welland its title of "The Rose City." The designer of the Welland memorial was Elizabeth Wyn Wood, a major player in the story of another monument that demonstrated the primacy of public will in the selection of commemoratives.

In 1924 a memorial committee was formed in Winnipeg and a competition for designs was announced shortly afterwards. The committee appointed a panel of experts, including architects and artists of national fame, to act as judges. In larger cities such as Winnipeg the choice of a design was made from an even greater number of entries than in smaller places, and in this case the judges looked at forty-seven models. One design was considered not only the best but was thought to be one of the finest examples they had ever seen of this type of work. The winner was Emmanual Hahn, a sculptor living in Toronto.

Plans to build the monument went ahead until Hahn's national origins were questioned. Could the name be German? Indeed it was. There was a further outcry from Winnipegers when it was learned that the artist had been born in Germany. Hahn had lived most of his life in Canada and had studied sculpture in Toronto, but so strong was the anti-German sentiment at the time that people felt it unfitting for him to execute a memorial to men who had been killed fighting Germans. Both of the city's newspapers as well as government and memorial committee members deplored the narrowness of the view, but it was obvious that popular opinion would not suffer Hahn's memorial to be built.

Sculptures by Hahn stand in a number of other places, including Springhill, Nova Scotia; Moncton, New Brunswick; Gaspé, Quebec; Meaford, Ontario; and Fernie, British Columbia. The sculpture in Westville, Nova Scotia, is the only one that was signed by Hahn, but his German birth had been made public elsewhere, even in Toronto where he lived and worked. Hahn designed monuments for the Thompson Company and its competitors often mentioned Hahn's origins in their sales pitch. This was another example of the lack of gentleness in the bidding for memorial contracts. In most other places, however, public opinion seems to have been more concerned with the appearance of the statues than with the accident of an artist's birthplace. In the end Hahn was paid the prize-money for winning the Winnipeg competition but the monument he designed was never built.

The issue of a memorial for Winnipeg was put to rest until 1927, when another competition was opened. This time it was stipulated that entrants be native Canadians or nationals of Allied countries in the Great War. Once again there was one design that quickly and unanimously captured the imagination of the judges. The winner, too, seemed perfect: Elizabeth Wyn Wood came from Orillia, Ontario. But controversy was not to be escaped that easily. The public soon discovered two things that became hot issues. First of all, Wyn Wood worked under her maiden name but was otherwise Mrs. Emmanual Hahn. Second, people found out that her design featured a nude male figure. She said it represented the vital spirit of the West. It is hard now to know which of these factors again led Winnipegers to reject a proposed memorial. They had already expressed their feelings about Hahn and this obviously clouded their view of his wife. Some even said that the design was probably his. As for the nude figure, however Elizabeth Wyn Wood saw the spirit of the West, it was clear that Winnipegers saw themselves with their clothes on. Again the prize money was paid for a statue that was never built. The Winnipeg memorial committee decided finally to opt for the next best entry, and since number two and three were so close and the third place design was by a local man, it was his entry that was chosen.

The events that unfolded in Winnipeg in the 1920s concerning the memorial do not reflect much credit on the city from our perspective. The stone shaft of the memorial that stands in the city today is adequately proportioned but could never be accused of striking originality. Wyn Wood's and Hahn's designs were both artistically superior. In *The Roar of the Twenties,* a critical look at life

Controversial Toronto artist Emmanual Hahn only signed one of his war memorial sculptures, this bronze statue in Westville, Nova Scotia. Street.

on the prairies in the decade after the First World War, James Grey found the
whole episode deplorable and indicative of deep prejudices that existed at the
time.[21] It is unlikely that even the people who held the narrow anti-German
attitude at the time would defend their actions today. The city would probably
just as soon forget the whole business. But it shows as well as anything that
public opinion, however reprehensible in hindsight and however unsophisticated in artistic taste, was the critical force in the decision of which monument
to build. In Winnipeg that opinion was such an independent factor that it operated outside the powers, such as newspapers and social leaders, that often ma-
nipulate it.

If there is any doubt about the necessity for popular consensus before a
monument could be built – any notion that a memorial could be erected on the
main street without anyone caring much – then those places without monuments should be considered. Why are there towns with no monument representing all those lost in wars? Why did some monuments not get built until
decades after the armistice of 1918? Despite general support in Canada for the
First World War, enthusiastic from all but the political left at first and grim as
time and casualty lists went on, the traditionally contentious forces in the nation continued to confront each other just beneath the surface. Those who sim-
ple-mindedly thought the war would bring easy unity ignored the depths of
division. Catholic-Protestant, labour-management, rural-urban, French-En-
glish, immigrant-native-born – none of these antagonisms were resolved. While
common danger tended to bring groups that were already close-knit even closer
together, the hardships of war, in many other cases, only aggravated the peren-
nial rifts.

Many groups and areas felt that they carried an unfair portion of the war
load. Speaking at the dedication of a plaque in a church in Exeter, Ontario, in
1920, the Bishop of Huron said that Anglicans played the biggest part in the
war. Writing about a proposed monument in the eastern Ontario village of Vankleek Hill, a committee member pointed to the number of local men who had
volunteered and said that "some parts of the country did not do their duty."[22]
Industrialists made fortunes from wartime contracts while workers got little but
long hours and commodity shortages. Labourers were first expected to enlist for
reasons of patriotism; they were then subjected to propaganda and finally co-
erced into uniform by conscription. Their wives and daughters were expected
to take their places in the factories and mills. The wealth of the upper class was
never conscripted the way a poor man's fortune – his sons – were. At the same
time the casualty rate among officers was proportionally higher than it was
among other ranks. These experiences left a bitterness between classes, groups,
and religions that was reflected in the stone of monuments or in the lack of it.

A fair proportion of the enlistment in Sydney, Nova Scotia, came from the
Catholic working class.[23] The only monument built soon after the First World

War in that steel mill city, however, was put up by the Orange Lodge and bears only the names of Protestant boys. It was not until after the Second World War that the Legion erected a general memorial. Orange-Catholic resentment was a fact of life in the Conception Bay region of Newfoundland, as well. The town of Carbonear was predominantly Protestant while neighbouring Harbour Grace was a Catholic community. Violence had erupted late in the nineteenth century with street battles growing out of rival parades and the scars were deep. A monument was built in Carbonear to a young Orangeman who had been shot dead in one of these riots in 1880, but no memorial commemorating the dead of the First World War was built in the 1920s or '30s in these places.

Waterloo, Ontario, was the centre of a pacifist Mennonite settlement. These German-speaking people had come from the United States as early as the 1790s. Subsequent German immigrants had gravitated to the area. A war of any kind, let alone a war with Germany, presented singular difficulties in relations between these people and their neighbours. There was never any indication of sympathy for the Kaiser's cause, but neither were German Canadians in places such as Waterloo over-anxious to fight. As the war progressed, propaganda about "Hun" barbarity and recruiting drives that stressed the cowardliness of those failing to enlist drove the wedge deeper. An angry mob, proclaiming pride in its English ancestry, took a statue of the Kaiser's grandfather from the German Club House and threw it in a lake in a 1917 demonstration. The mood did not mellow for some time after the war. A Mr. Wells of the Waterloo Parks Board wrote to Ottawa asking for a captured German gun to display in the city. He explained that many local men had enlisted, but the fact was that it was a German settlement and "they" and "their children" needed to see a big gun captured by Canadians from "the army that had so long been the pride of their race."[24] Needless to say, no monument to the fallen of the Great War was erected in Waterloo until long after the war's end.

Farmers all over the country came to question the war, though the ones in Quebec were most organized and are best remembered. They were expected to feed both grain and sons to the war effort and the feat became more difficult as time went on. Reaction against this dilemma surfaced most readily where previous grievances simmered. West Elgin County, in southwestern Ontario, had been the home for several generations of dispossessed settlers from the Scottish Highlands, nurtured in their resentment of English domination. Monuments are conspicuous by their absence in a cluster of towns and villages in the area. The economist John Kenneth Galbraith wrote in retrospect about the region where he had grown up. In his book *The Scotch* he may have intended humour rather than history, yet it may be a case of the true word said in jest: "During the First World War, when young Canadians were volunteering enthusiastically for euthanasia on the Western Front, the Scotch regarded the whole enterprise with reserve."[25] When they did fight, men from the areas where the war was less than popular could do so with distinction. Two men from a single town in rural Quebec and one from Elgin County won Victoria Crosses. But rural opposition showed up in lower enlistment at the time and, where the wounds of intra-communal tension did not heal, in the absence of representative memorials after the war.

There are many factors inherent in the nature of war and its aftermath that might have pulled communities apart. It is hardly surprising that there are examples of towns where sufficient co-operation could not be found to allow monuments to be built in public places. What is surprising is that despite centrifugal forces, the requisite degree of agreement was reached in the vast majority of Canadian communities. It indicates a remarkable ability and willingness on the part of a diverse people to bridge gaps and combine their efforts in a common desire to commemorate a common loss.

The phenomenal combining of community effort is most striking where it is seen against the backdrop of Canada's most persistent dividing line. Monuments in much of Quebec, New Brunswick, and in parts of Ontario are inscribed, "*Nos Morts – Our Dead.*" Some bilingual inscriptions are much longer. In Caraquet, New Brunswick, where the sounds of French and English mingle in the taverns like the smell of beer and *patates frites,* the monument reads, *"Dédié à la mémoire des vallants enfants de notre district morts au champ d'honneur."* – "Dedicated to the memory of the brave sons of our district who gave their lives in the war." The significant sentiment is that it is always "our dead" and *"notre district."* In St. Lambert, Quebec, across the river from Montreal, the English part of the inscription comes first, while in neighbouring Longueuil it is the French that precedes the English. The bilingual inscription becomes multilingual in the eastern Ontario county of Glengarry. There the Scots settlers were not descended from evicted crofters as in Elgin County, but from Loyalists, and so they felt the traditional attachment to the British Crown. In Alexandria, Gaelic joins French and English on the town's monument: *"Ha Cuinhuich Agaim – Je Me Souviens – I Remember."*

An incalculable amount of work had to be done in organizing people, raising funds, and sustaining the efforts to build memorials. Most of what went on remains invisible unless we dig deeply into what records or personal recollections remain. Much of the effort went unnoticed even at the time. When the moment came to unveil the statue, cairn, obelisk, or other form of monument, the true extent of its popular appeal was revealed in a momentary flash. The account of what happened in Piapot, Saskatchewan, as reported in the Regina *Leader* of November 17, 1933 is typical: "From early morning until late at night crowds came into the town from all corners for the purpose of taking part in the dedication ceremony." The Brampton, Ontario, *Conservator* of July 5, 1928, called the monument unveiling the "greatest moment in the long life of the town." Almost identical words were used in the *North Battleford News* of October 23, 1924, to describe the dedication there. Another indication of how seriously monument unveilings were taken can be gained from the situation that occurred in St. Catharines, Ontario, in August 1927. The popular Prince of Wales came to town to dedicate the memorial but when he showed up in a "lounge suit," what we now think of suitable dress for formal occasions, instead of a uniform or other more formal attire, it was noted with chagrin in the *St. Catharines Standard*. In October 1921, the *London Free Press* reported that, "for the first time in the history of the Township of East Nissouri, the whole countryside turned out en masse to attend the unique and impressive celebration of the unveiling of the soldiers' monument in Kintor." In Regina, where the population in the 1920s was about thirty-five thousand, and in Halifax, where perhaps fifty-eight thousand people lived, the crowds attending the monument unveilings were estimated at over ten thousand.[26]

The heavily-attended dedication gatherings are the final indication of the depth and breadth of support that was accorded to monuments. They are the hard currency of a community's spirit. Consensus was not easily reached and is the more remarkable in that it was not verbally expressed. The feelings that people shared were spoken mostly through the silent words carved on the stone of the memorials located in the centres of most towns, cities, and villages in Canada.

Crowds at monument unveilings such as this one in Brantford, Ontario were extrordinary. PAO.

FIVE
The World-Old Custom

A crown reflowering on the tombs of kings,
Who earned their trimph and have claimed their sleep.
Duncan Campbell Scott: "In the Country Churchyard"

In the rural Nova Scotia town of Stewiacke two streets named Main and Kitchener come together at an odd angle. Around the open space formed by their meeting stand the town hall, the bank, the railway station, the post office, and the general store. Some time after the First World War the citizens of Stewiacke built a memorial on the gore between the two streets. It consists of a tall, tapering stone shaft supported on four stone pillars. Around the same time, thousands of kilometres away, the people of Princeton, British Columbia, built a small stone pyramid in the centre of their town. On the monument in Princeton are the names of thirty men. In Stewiacke forty-one names are carved in stone.

These monuments have been given places of honour in the heart of

There is no inscription on this memorial in Stewiacke, Nova Scotia that tells you what it commemorates. Street.

(opposite) In the Victoria, British Columbia suburb of Oak Bay there are often fresh flowers placed in front of the memorial. The same poignant care is shown in many other places. Shipley.

The ancient forms of arch and pyramid in Princeton, British Columbia invite the passerby to pause and think. Shipley.

their communities. They are respectfully set off from the busy streets by borders of trees and grass. You approach the monument in Princeton through an arched gate. On the gate are written the words "Lest We Forget." Similar monuments, usually afforded an equally honoured place, appeared spontaneously in hundreds of Canadian communities in the years that followed the Great War of 1914-18. Towns that did not build them in the 1920s or '30s generally did so after the Second World War.

For the families and close friends of the men and women who had been killed, the monuments had a particular function. They were "designed to afford many bereaved the opportunity to express visibly their sorrow."[1] Even after all these years that is still true. Fresh flowers are placed in front of many memorials every day. The significance of monuments, however, was not limited to the feelings of those who suffered an immediate loss. It was entire communities that had erected the cairns and statues. The monuments were built of durable materials and were obviously intended to last beyond the lifetimes of the dead soldiers' family and friends, and to speak to something greater than personal loss. From those who had not been deprived of one close to them, from those too young to remember, and from future generations, memorials were intended to elicit a more general feeling of reverence. It was hoped that the viewer would pause in front of the memorial, for a moment at least, to consider the dead and the implications of their passing. The German word for monument is *Denkmal,* and it expresses this intent more clearly. It means, literally, "think-time."

The shock of losing so many young people in war had a deep impact on Canadian society. The need to remember their service and their sacrifice, and the desire to be inspired by their selfless example, was clear to those who were left. The need to remember all those who died was also a common feeling that brought together most elements in our communities. But people knew that memories would fade with time. They knew that old and new frictions would eventually pull them in different directions. Thus, while they were united and while their memories were vivid, people built permanent monuments. These symbols of common sorrow and shared beliefs would help to summon back these important ideas when time and forgetfulness and dissension threatened to work their mischief on the community.

Sociologists have speculated about the physical symbols that people build to represent their ideas.[2] It may be that the phenomenal spread of memorials throughout Canada was an answer to some fundamental human need. For the people who collected money for memorials or piled up the stones they had gathered, there was no theory, however, there was no conscious understanding of sociological imperatives. Canadians built memorials out of their instinctive knowledge that it was important for them, and for those who came after, to remember what had happened in their time.

The purpose of the monument in Princeton, British Columbia, is made clear in its inscription. It reads, "Erected to the memory of the men of the Princeton district who fell in the Great War." Inscriptions concerning the memory of the dead are even more explicit on other monuments in the country. The words of the British poet Wilfred Owen appear in both French and English on the memorial in Drummondville, Quebec:

> *Au coucher du soleil et quand se levera l'aurore,*
> *Nous évoquerons leur mémoire.*
> At the going down of the sun and in the morning,
> We will remember them.

In Rouleau, Saskatchewan, we read that the memorial was "erected as a tribute to the valour of the men of this district who, counting honour more precious than life or freedom, risked their lives in the service of King and Country in the Great War, 1914-18, and in honoured memory of those who fell whose names are inscribed hereon."

Stewiacke, Nova Scotia, however, is one of the many places where the inscription tells us nothing at all about the intent of the monument. "Died Overseas" is all it says above its list of names. Other memorials bear only the simple legends, "Our Glorious Dead," "Remember," or *"Pro Patria."* The National Memorial in Ottawa has only the dates "1914-1918," to which was later added the dates of the Second World War and the Korean conflict. The memorial in Hastings, Ontario, shows names of several men but has no other words carved on it at all.

Yet monuments are able to communicate their message by their form alone.[3] For the same reason they can have an impact on the passerby who is too far away to read what words may be carved on them. This prior understanding is the result of the repeated use of the same monument forms throughout history.[4] When the people of Stewiacke, Nova Scotia, and Princeton, British Columbia, built monuments in the centres of their towns, they were carrying on an extremely old tradition. An exploration of that tradition, which the Toronto *Globe* of January 5, 1907 called a "world-old custom," helps to explain the provocative power of simple piles of stones.

The ancestors of Canadian memorials are ancient and the pedigree of even the simplest form is impressive. The memorial in Princeton is essentially nothing more than a pile of stones. There are at the very least two hundred other monuments in Canada that take roughly the same form.[5] Given the nature of a rock-strewn landscape and the desire to mark a spot, the cairn was an instinctive solution. In the Bible, when the Israelites ended forty years in the wilderness and crossed the Jordan River into the Promised Land, they did exactly the same thing. They set up a pile of stones to be "a memorial unto the Children of Israel for ever"(Josh. 4:7). A verse from the account of this event as told in the Book of Joshua was a favourite of clergymen at the dedication of Canadian monuments. "In the future your children will ask, what is the meaning of these stones?" The Bible has numerous other references to memorials. A little further on in the Book of Joshua we learn that the Jews defeated an enemy and burned his city. Afterwards, they "raised a great heap of stones that remaineth to this day"(Josh. 10:29). After his visionary dream Jacob "set up a pillar in the place, . . . even a pillar of stone"(Gen. 35:14). The altars that were used in the Bible for sacrificing offerings to God were also made by piling up stones. The Law of Moses, as stated in Exodus 20:25 and Deuteronomy 37:5-6, contains fairly precise instructions for building these altars.

Our present picture of what the ancient biblical memorials looked like may not have much to do with an accurate rendering of Hebrew history, but may well owe more to the imaginations of the nineteenth-century engravers who illustrated the old family Bibles that are the source of our impressions. The cairns in places such as Princeton may look no more like Joshua's monument than children dressed up in bathrobes for a Christmas pageant look like shepherds. But the important thing is that something similar to what we now know as a stone cairn was being built in ancient times. In the Canadian context people wanted to associate their monument building with models from sacred writings; the intent was to communicate a reverent mood and the use of biblical forms, as they were understood, embodied this attitude.

The mysterious people who in-habited the British Isles and northern France before the time of written his-tory were responsible for some of the world's most enduring monuments. Because those areas are the root soil for much of Canada's cultural inheri-tance, it is not surprising that some of our memorials echo the form of the "menhirs," or standing stones. The original function of Stonehenge and similar sites is still a matter of schol-arly speculation. That they had some religious purpose is almost certain. By the time the influence of Christianity was felt in Britain and France, the standing stones were simply accepted as having a sacred significance and were adopted as sites of worship by the new religion.

Some of the ancient menhirs were single tall stones set upright. Others consisted of several upright stones with another slab balanced on the top of them. The memorial in Stewiacke has both of these elements. One piece of stone rests on four pillars. On top of that rises a single shaft.

Many monuments, especially in the larger cities such as Montreal, Toronto, Calgary, and Vancouver, had as their immediate model the White-hall Cenotaph in London, England. The memorial in London, Ontario, is

The similarity between memorial stones like this one in Chatsworth, Ontario and the old standing stones in Northern Europe is not accidental. Shipley.

Toronto's cenotaph in front of Old City Hall is typical of those found in the metropolises. Street.

an exact scaled-down copy. The English architect Sir Edwin Lutyens designed the Whitehall monument as well as some of those for the battlefields on the Continent. Lutyens was obsessed with the notion of durability, so it was natural that he turned for inspiration to the oldest monuments that survive in Britain and France. While the Whitehall Cenotaph is constructed of a number of smoothly polished blocks of stone and has sculptural detail added to its surface, it is essentially a simple, massive, firmly-based pillar of rock not at all unlike the stones that have stood in the English and French countryside since before the Romans came. The Canadian examples of this type of memorial are no less solid.[6]

A form of monument that is even older than the cairns spoken of in the Bible or the standing stones of northern Europe is the Egyptian pyramid. The five-thousand-year-old originals are still standing and the miniature versions in Princeton, British Columbia, Brighton, Ontario, and Goldboro, Nova Scotia, are all unmistakable descendants. Another monument of Egyptian origin is the obelisk. It is a variation of the pyramidal shape that was considered by the ancients to be endowed with magical powers. The first pyramids may have been representations of the sun's rays streaming down through the clouds after a rain. The obelisk is a very steep-sided pyramid which is cut off at the top and capped by a smaller pyramid. The stone shaft atop the memorial in Stewiacke is an obelisk.

Each of the other half dozen or so basic forms of monuments found in Canada has a line of progenitors that stretches back over the centuries to Europe. Statues of gods and mortals were set up in public squares by the Greeks and Romans. Figures of kings and saints guarded the entrances to medieval Christian cathedrals. The soldiers on so many of our monuments and the winged angels that make occasional appearances follow in this tradition of memorial statuary. The Romans also built triumphal arches to commemorate their victories. Their French, German, and English heirs in Europe each built triumphal arches in their time. The modest arched gate in Princeton is one of numerous memorial portals in Canada. When it came to commemorating those humble citizens who could not afford great tombs or mausoleums, the Greeks were among the first to mark their graves with small, rectangular slabs of stone. On these they inscribed the name and even the picture of the deceased. The Greek stele, or head-stone, was the forerunner of the grave markers we use in our cemeteries as well as one of the forms we have adopted as a war memorial.

Monuments are able to communi-cate a reverent, respectful, and thoughtful mood not only because the forms have remained unchanged for centuries, but because they have con-sistently been used for the same things. They have either been tombs or grave markers, commemorations of great people or celebrations of impor-tant historical events. Through this association of certain shapes repeat-edly used for specific purposes, monu-ments have become a kind of lan-guage. The language is not only un-derstood by European cultures and their offsprings but by other, more dis-tant cultures as well. We stand silently in front of the huge Easter Island heads or West Coast totem poles, sens-ing that they have some deep and sig-nificant meaning. They demand that we stop and think.

Flesherton, Ontario and many other communities adopted the simple grave marker of ancient Greece. Street.

This kind of communication is not at all obscure. It has many parallels in other contexts. When we are watching a movie, certain musical backgrounds will alert us that the next scene is going to be suspenseful, violent, or amusing. The black border around a newspaper notice tells us that is is a death announce-ment before we begin to read it. We do not need to see the words "Stop," or *Arrêt,* to know the meaning of the eight-sided sign in the distance. Understand-ing the meaning of certain music, colours, and forms is a matter of cultural conditioning.[7] These things achieve their communicative force through habit-ual use.

Memorials in Canada look not only like the ancient models from which they are derived, but often very much like one another. Substitute the sea of brine for a sea of grass and the obelisk in Crystal City, Manitoba, would be all but indistinguishable from the one in Port aux Basque, Newfoundland. Both are much like the one in Stewiacke, Nova Scotia. The marble soldier in Terrebonne, Quebec, has dozens of near-twins, including the statue in Taber, Alberta. The stone pyramid near Greenwood, British Columbia, resembles the one in Princeton because it was probably made by the same mason. But the one in Brighton, Ontario, is thousands of kilometres away and it is similar simply because there are only so many ways to make a pyramid.

Some people have lamented this uniformity. They have criticized what they see as a lack of originality in monument design. One art historian referred to Canadian memorials as "a subject generally treated with depressing banality."[8] From time to time the controversy about originality has focused on particular monuments. One such battle was joined in the 1960s by a group in Victoria, British Columbia. An art historian from the University of Victoria said of the memorial in Oak Bay, "If a pastry cook had been hired to contract the Uplands War Memorial, then I would praise it as a great work; but an artist made it, so I won't praise it as great work because it isn't." In answer to the unfavourable comments on the Oak Bay or Uplands statue, a Victoria columnist ventured the assumption that critics "do not have the emotional background, whatever their artistic qualifications, to appraise a work of this nature."[9]

The laurel branch carved from stone on the base of the memorial in Fredericton, New Brunswick is part of the age-old pattern of symbolism. Shipley.

The art critics were viewing each memorial as an opportunity for original sculptural expression. But to criticize Canadian monuments for being artistically unoriginal is to misunderstand their function in society. The art of the monument is not the art of innovation. The challenge that designing a monument presents to the artist or craftsman is to create something of beauty and sensitivity within the very strict stylistic conditions imposed by tradition. He has to work from a given repertoire of forms that will inspire within the viewers the emotional intent of the memorial.

The great majority of monuments in Canada were built some time ago and conform to one or other of the ancient models. Still, there have been attempts to break away from the traditional forms. Public acceptance has always been the arbiter in these cases. The original plan for Viljo Revell's Toronto City Hall called for a cenotaph to be placed in the adjoining square. It was to be the work of Revell's friend Henry Moore.[10] It soon became obvious from public discussion that people in Toronto would not have related well to a memorial in Moore's style. Moore's *Archer* was eventually placed in Nathan Phillips Square, but it was not paid for by the public or the city and it was not dedicated as a memorial.[11] In the early 1960s, at about the same time that Toronto's new City Hall was being built, Quebec sculptor Arman Vaincourt created a war memorial for the city of Chicoutimi. While its style caused some controversy as well, it was eventually accepted. This was probably because people could relate to it as a war memorial in traditional symbolic terms. It was said to resemble a large gun.[12]

Some war memorials in Canada are exceptionally beautiful sculptures. Whatever many others lack in terms of pure artistry, all of them together form a particular expression of an ancient and perhaps even imperative human activity. The statues, cairns, and pillars in the centres of our towns and cities link us to our past, and express our inheritance as clearly as any element in our physical or cultural landscape.

SIX
Symbolic of Canadian Ideals

And if you 'as to die,
As it sometimes 'appens why,
Far better die a 'ero than a skunk . . .
    Robert Service: "Funk"

Memorials have been built by people in every part of the world, and the origins of monumental forms stretch back to the beginnings of human society. Yet memorials in Canada, in spite of the similarities to older and distant ones, have their own distinctive expression. They have evolved meanings that grew out of ancient traditions but speak of modern concerns and ideas.

    The primary function of memorials is the visible expression of grief at the loss of fallen soldiers. Beyond this, monuments carry a number of meanings with none ringing more clearly than the sense of pride in a country. Indeed, the building of monuments in the past often marked a people's rite of passage into nationhood. Joshua's cairn by the Jordan signified the establishment of the Hebrew nation in Palestine. Much later, when Europe began to emerge from the Dark Ages, cities and countries as we know them today took shape. Church spires appeared above the old walls in an impressive style that announced a new order. "The high Gothic cathedrals of France . . . are truly national monuments, the tangible expressions of that merging of religious and patriotic fervour."[1] Memorial towers at the University of Toronto, in Aurora, Woodbridge, and Simcoe, Ontario, and in Wainwright, Alberta, echo those former declarations of national identity in a Canadian context. Men from every part of Canada stood shoulder to shoulder on the battlefields of the First World War. The country had overcome many tensions at home and had united to make a proportionally massive contribution to the Allied cause. "That such a war record would carry Canada to full autonomy had been foreseen by Sir Robert Borden, and so it

(opposite) Distinctive Canadian emblems on the collar and sleeve of the soldier at Shelburne, Ontario clearly mark his nationality. Street.

proved. A separate Canadian signature on the Peace Treaty signified that the status of nationhood had been achieved."[2]

Monuments in communities from coast to coast celebrate the achievement in their symbolism. On the stone gate leading into the memorial gardens in West Vancouver, British Columbia, the maple leaf figures prominently in the design. The national emblem is seen again on other monuments across the country. The maple leaf had been the principal element in the badges of many battalions of the Canadian Expeditionary Force overseas. In places such as Revenna, Ontario, and St-Lambert, Quebec, and in most other instances where sculptures of Canadian soldiers were used on memorials, the maple leaf insignia is clearly visible on the caps and collars of the figures. Some statues, such as the one in Fort William, Ontario, also have distinctive Canadian unit patches. These were pieces of coloured felt that were cut in various shapes and sewn to the arms of the uniforms to identify division, brigade, and battalion.

National feeling was also displayed in the ceremonies dedicating and commemorating the monuments themselves. The June 29 Regina *Leader* reports that Ogema, Saskatchewan, unveiled its monument in 1923 and was the first of many places to use a Canadian Ensign rather than a Union Jack. At North Battleford, Saskatchewan, in 1924, according to the April 23 *North Battleford News*, "O Canada" was sung in place of "God Save the King" at the unveiling of the cenotaph. A poetic prayer read by Rev. John H. Lea at an annual memorial service in front of the monument in Cartwright, Manitoba, reached back to capture some of the fervour that surrounded memorial building:

> *O God of all the many lands,*
> *we lift our hearts to thee*
> *for this fair land our Canada,*
> *a country wide and free . . .*
> *We thank thee for the sacrifice*
> *of daring men of old,*
> *for faith to cross uncharted seas,*
> *for dreams to make men bold . . .*
> *We thank thee that from many lands*
> *with varied gifts they came*
> *to pledge their love and loyalty*
> *where scarlet maples flame . . .*[3]

According to the Regina *Leader* of June 15, 1923, when Major M. A. MacPherson spoke at the dedication of the statue in Wolseley, Saskatchewan, he said that while the memorial was a tribute to local men, it was also built in homage to all Canadians who fell.

Symbolic statements of national pride have continued in monuments built in more recent years. A large maple leaf made of wire and foil was added to the top of an older cairn in Two Hills, Alberta. In the village of Oakdale near Brantford, Ontario, the Legion built a large concrete war memorial in the shape of a map of Canada. Terence Lyster, a Vancouver architect, designed a new cenotaph for Qualicum Beach, British Columbia, in 1973. Constructed of metal and local logs, the memorial is a stylized maple leaf and embodies allusions to other traditional symbols, including the Union Jack, the fleur-de-lis, and the eternal flame.

The significance of Canadian war monuments as symbols of a new national awareness is demonstrated further by the prominent positions they occupy in most communities. The country had seen disasters involving great loss of life before the First World War and was to experience them again. Others, besides soldiers, had died either in significant numbers in the service of the public, and these losses had led people to erect commemorations. Montreal and Toronto have memorials to victims of the frightful cholera epidemics of the nineteenth century. Memorials in Toronto and Halifax cemeteries remember those lost in the wrecks of the *Empress of Ireland* and the *Titanic*. There are monuments to firemen who died in the line of duty in both Catholic and Protestant cemeteries in Montreal. No industry has been more consistently dangerous than mining and the collieries under Springhill, Nova Scotia, claimed more lives locally than the trenches of Flanders: in 1891, 125 men died in a single day's cave-in, while the four years between 1914 and 1918 took 81 of Springhill's sons. There are miners' memorials not only in Springhill but in Westville, Nova Scotia, New Waterford, Cape Breton Island, and other mining towns as well. In each of these cases, however, it is the war memorial that occupies the more prominent position in the community because it has a meaning that goes beyond the commemoration of the dead.

The national sentiment expressed by war memorials was particularly evident in border areas. Parallel to Rainy River, which marks the Canada-US boundary in northwestern Ontario, there are six cenotaphs in the space of ninety kilometres. They form a kind of second demarcation line. The March 18, 1923 edition of the Regina *Leader* reports that in North Portal, Saskatchewan, one of the requirements for the location of the monument was that it be close to and visible from the border crossing. A letter written in the 1920s to an Ontario parliamentary commission on memorials urged that the province build a monument close to one of the Niagara border crossings: that way it would be one of the first things visitors from the United States would see.[4] In St. Stephen, New Brunswick, and Fort Erie, Ontario, the soldiers' memorial is one of the first sights to greet anyone entering the country from the American side. At Brockville, Ontario, there is a larger-than-life bronze Canuck in the act of lobbing a hand grenade across the St. Lawrence River into New York State.

Newfoundland did not become part of Canada until 1949, but its experience during the First World War was very similar to the other provinces'. The caribou is the symbol both of the Royal Newfoundland Regiment and Newfoundland itself. Statues of soldiers like the one in Bay Roberts feature the caribou badge in the same way that the maple leaf is found on the mainland. In St. John's, at Bowring Park, there is a life-sized statue of a caribou. Several other versions of the same sculpture mark the battlefields in France and Belgium where the Newfoundland Regiment fought.

The cultural mosaic was part of the reality of Canada long before promoting it became official government policy. Along with a national Canadian identity, therefore, monuments in certain places also reflected various cultural traditions and ethnic distinctions.

In Pugwash, Nova Scotia, the street signs are in Scots Gaelic as well as English and the town's memorial statue is a kilted soldier. Judique, Digby, and Chester are among other Nova Scotia or "New Scotland" communities with Highlanders on their monuments. In New Glasgow, Nova Scotia, the statue is a piper. The Gaelic tradition shows up as well in the numerous Celtic crosses that serve as memorials. Modern versions of this ancient form are found in Sackville, New Brunswick, Port Credit, Ontario, and Haney, British Columbia, while an up-to-date neon Celtic cross serves as a memorial in Hinton, Alberta.

The Sons of England Benevolent Society was a co-operative group organized to look after the emergency needs of members in the era before there were many public social programs. After the First World War the society built a number of memorials to honour its members who had lost their lives overseas. The traditional lion symbol of England is included in these memorials in Toronto and Guelph, Ontario, and elsewhere.

In the north shore New Brunswick village of Grande-Anse, the yellow star of Acadia appears in the stone work in front of the monument. Acadians had long before suffered expulsion from their lands in the Maritimes, but had returned and re-established themselves. In the First and Second World Wars they went out to defend their old homeland and showed the growing pride they had in their own particular culture by including its symbol in this monument. At the other end of the country lived a more recently arrived ethnic minority who were to live through an expulsion not unlike the Acadian deportation. A great many Japanese Canadians served with distinction and gave their lives during the First World War.[5] The monument in Vancouver's Stanley Park that commemorates them was built in 1920. It is striking in view of the fact that during the Second World War Japanese Canadians were deprived of all their civil rights, had their property confiscated, and were interned.

Polish, Ukrainian, Hungarian, Jewish, and Russian immigrants to Canada have built memorials in such places as St. Catharines and Toronto, Ontario, Rawden, Quebec, and Winnipeg, Manitoba. These monuments generally in-

In Winnipeg's All Saints Cemetery stands a monument dedicated to the memory of Ukrainian and Ukrainian-Canadian war victims. This is one of many memorials in Canada remembering members of ethnic communities other than British and French. Shipley.

clude both Canadian emblems and the symbols of the old country as well as inscriptions in both English and the particular national language and script. They remember those from the specific community who were killed while serving in the Canadian Forces and those relatives and friends who fought in the old countries.

Many people who immigrated to Canada in the years before the First World War had to return to their former home countries when the armies were mobilized in 1914. Memorials in Montreal, Quebec, and St. Boniface, Manitoba, commemorate these conscripts and show statues of men in the uniforms of Belgium and France.

The Italian community in Toronto commemorated the losses of the First World War in a rather unique way. They commissioned a large bronze plaque showing the English nurse-heroine Edith Cavell, who was executed by the Germans for allegedly helping Allied prisoners escape. This tribute to one victim of the war from one ethnic group in Canada perhaps represents as well as any the sentiments that unite all the people in the country.

Just as the traditional nationalistic expression implied by Old World monuments has been given a distinctly Canadian voice in the country's memorials, so the other meanings of statues and arches have been changed to fit our experience. Monuments had celebrated victory in war from the very earliest times. The hieroglyphic inscription on an ancient Egyptian obelisk reads, "Rameses II, lord of Kingly and Queenly royalty, guardian of Egypt, and chastiser of foreign lands."[6] The beautiful temple of Athena Nike, the wingless victory, on the Acropolis of Athens commemorates the Persian defeat by the Greeks at the battle of Salamis Bay in 480 B.C. Trajan's Column in Rome signifies military victories, as does Nelson's Column built hundreds of years later in London's Trafalgar Square.

In the last one hundred and fifty years, however, a different sensitivity about war has arisen in Western society. A wounded lion figure was carved from the living rock in a park in Lucerne, Switzerland, about 1820. It was probably the first memorial that commemorated not a victory but the loss of soldiers. It was dedicated to the Swiss Guards who were killed defending the Tuilleries Palace during the French Revolution.[7] Another lion statue in Reading, England, remembers the three hundred men of the local regiment who were wiped out in a rather conclusive defeat in Afghanistan in 1880. Numerous memorials appeared in France following that country's humiliating defeat in a war with Prussia in 1870. The most significant of these was Auguste Rodin's work from the 1890s, *The Burghers of Calais*. The sculpture represents an incident that occurred three hundred years before, but it captured the contemporary French feeling. It was intended as a "tribute to heroism in defeat."[8]

In Canada the monuments built after the First World War are almost universally concerned with the suffering of war and the grief of losing young men.

(left) The insignia of the R.C.A.F. and several army regiments appear on the monument outside the parish church in Montmagny, Quebec. Symbols such as the fleur-de-lis on the second badge from the top and the beaver in the bottom isignia are themselves part of the Canadian identity. Shipley.

(right) The Celtic Cross that serves as the memorial in Haney, British Columbia speaks of Scottish and Irish heritage but a maple leaf is woven into the traditional design. Shipley.

Seldom do they even mention victory. The statue in Lethbridge, Alberta, is typical. It shows a soldier in mourning and the inscription reads, "In honor of those whose names endure, . . . they have passed on leaving the heritage of a glorious memory." The cenotaph in Montreal pays tribute to the soldiers not for victory but for bringing "honour and peace." Even in the handful of instances where there are statues of soldiers in a warlike posture the inscriptions still speak of "supreme sacrifice" and say things such as "they died that we might live."[9]

"Resting on Arms Reversed" is the military term for the position of mourning represented by the memorial statue in Lethbridge, Alberta. Shipley.

Where weapons are part of monuments their symbolic meaning often de-emphasizes the warlike. In the village of Bethany, Ontario, three rifles lean together the way soldiers leave them when they are asleep. Monuments such as the one in Fredericton, New Brunswick, have carved representations of military equipment. There is a helmet, rifle, bayonet, and belt, but unlike ancient monuments such as Trajan's Column which showed the victors carrying home the captured arms of a defeated enemy, the gear here belongs to one of Canada's own soldiers. It is not the booty of war but the discarded equipment of our own dead who have no more need of it.

At Bethany, Ontario rifles are stacked on the monument in the way they would have been left by soldiers when they were asleep. Street.

In the Old World war memorials usually honoured individual heroes, kings, and leaders. There were monuments to Roman emperors, French generals, and English admirals. The tradition was carried on in America, where there were statues of Bolivar erected in the former Spanish colonies he liberated; to Washington and Civil War generals in the United States; Wolfe, Montcalm, Nelson, and Brock in Canada, as well as home-grown heroes such as Colonel Williams in Port Hope, Ontario. But the rise of humanism and romanticism led people to commemorate unsuccessful and costly struggles as well as victories, the same way that the rise of democratic ideas prompted people to remember the common soldier as well as the general. The Arc de Triomphe in Paris commemorates Napoleon's victories but includes Rude's sculptural group *La Marseillaise,* which honours the volunteers in France's post revolutionary wars.

When memorials were built in Canadian communities after the First World War only a few took the form of individual portraits. The statues were almost always of the average citizen soldier. The names of the dead were in alphabetical order or in the order of the dates when they were killed. Sometimes the officers' names came first but equality was the general rule. Even in places like Almonte, Ontario, where the statue did represent a specific individual, it was called "The Volunteer": Alexander Rosamond was considered typical and the memorial remembered not just him but all those from the community who fell.

The writer and critic Margaret Atwood mentions Northrop Frye and Robin Matthews as other observers of Canadian culture who believe, as she does, that "the pull of the native tradition is not in the direction of individual heroes at all, but in the direction of the collective heroes."[10] The citizen soldier gazing fixedly down over our towns and cities from his pedestal is the typical Canadian collective hero. As with heroes who were memorialized in earlier times, our soldier has come to represent things beyond whatever personal qualities he may have possessed.

There is an impressive equestrian statue of a mercenary general named Bartolommeo Colleoni in Venice. The Renaissance Venetians did not necessarily revere Colleoni, but the statue, which the English poet Shelly described as having "the sneer of cold command," reminded them of their powerful position in the world.[11] Michelangelo's statue of David appealed similarly to the Florentines, who regarded themselves as political giant killers. The present leaders of the Soviet Union allow Peter the Great to continue to ride his bronze charger for the glory of Russia even though the notion of kingship is now officially frowned on.

Our soldier statues and other memorials are intended to remind us of the principles that were fought for or demonstrated in the wars. The words "Humanity, Endurance, Duty and Sacrifice" are inscribed on the four sides of the memorial at Oxdrift in northern Ontario. In Rimby, Alberta, the word in large letters on the memorial is "Valour." The memorial inscription in Richibucto, New Brunswick, speaks of men *"qui ont donné leur vie pour La Liberté."*

Although the statue at Almonte, Ontario is a portrait, it is intended to represent all local "Volunteers." Street.

Symbolic of Canadian Ideals

CANADIANS demand in manufactured products a high standard of excellence in keeping with Canada's National Ideals.

The McLaughlin—"Canada's Standard Car"—is symbolic of these ideals because of its beauty, efficiency and popularity.

Built in Canada by Canadian workmen for service on Canadian highways, McLaughlin cars by their exceptional service have won an enviable reputation among discriminating motorists.

SEND FOR A CATALOG.

The McLAUGHLIN MOTOR CAR CO.,
OSHAWA, ONTARIO.   Limited

McLAUGHLIN MASTER SIX H-6-49

McLAUGHLIN MOTOR CARS—REVISED PRICES

Model 63, Light Six	$1760.00
Model 45, Master Six (special finish)	$2440.00
Model 49, Seven-passenger (special finish)	$2850.00

F. O. B. VICTORIA

This advertisement appeared in the Victoria Daily Colonist *on November 9, 1919. It shows an artist's conception of a memorial before more than a handful existed in the country. National Library, Ottawa.*

Advertising can be a good indicator of popular trends. Businesses generally do not spend their public relations dollars in ways that are out of step with current sentiments. On November 10, 1921 a promotion for McLaughlin Motor Cars appeared in the *Daily Colonist* in Victoria, British Columbia. The Master Six, H-6-49 convertible touring car was pictured in front of a monument. The obelisk had a maple leaf on it and was surrounded by statues of soldiers. One of the statues held a Canadian ensign. "Symbolic of Canadian Ideals," the ad began, and went on to say, "Canadians demand in manufactured products a high standard of excellence in keeping with Canada's National Ideals."

The atmosphere in the country is considerably different now than it was in 1921. Canadians are not as likely to declare succinctly what their ideals are or to think of the war dead as exemplifying their best principles. But the memorials with all their symbolic meaning intact are still there. They are part of the visual fabric of our communities as a piece of contemporary advertising shows. A wine producer in the area of the popular tourist town of Niagara-on-the-Lake, Ontario, uses a local picture on the label of one of its vintages. The picture is of the war memorial that stands in the middle of the main street. Perhaps the ideals represented by monuments have simply become an accepted feature in the centre of our culture, the way the memorials have blended naturally into the shape of our towns.

The Caribou is emblematic of Newfoundland and appears as part of many monuments in that province including this arch in the settlement of Deer Lake. Shipley.

SEVEN
At the Mercy of Public Taste

The monuments so far as done by art,
George Laing has not been wanting on his part.
Will the Ranter in the Halifax *Morning Journal*, July 25, 1860.

Until fairly recently the story of public sculpture in Canada has been, for the most part, the story of war memorials. There are some outdoor religious carvings in Quebec, some statues of politicians, a few enthroned figures of Queen Victoria, and the odd bronzed explorer found mostly on the grounds around parliament buildings and in the parks of major cities. Where there are statues or monuments of any kind outside the commercial and political capitals, they are generally commemorations of the War of 1812, the Fenian Raids, the North-West Rebellion, the Boer War, and, most often, the First World War.

Sculpture, and especially commemorative monumental sculpture, has never enjoyed much of a critical reputation in Canada. One artist called it the "Cinderella" of the arts in this country.[1] If that is true, then the establishment critics have played the part of the ugly sisters and no handsome prince has yet come forward to rescue traditional Canadian statuary from continued abuse.[2]

This rather unfortunate situation has come about largely as a result of how public monuments were chosen. Committees, usually composed of citizens and politicians, picked from among the submissions of artists, architects, and monument companies, and the standards to be met by these submissions were often set by committees themselves. "From the time of Michelangelo," one Canadian artist complained, "committees have thwarted the sculptor."[3] Alfred Howell was one of the many sculptors working in Canada who was unwillingly dragged into the public controversy over a monument. In Saint John, New Brunswick, the city council wanted Howell to ally himself with them in a debate over the location of the monument. They were at war with the Women's Christian Temperance Union (WCTU) because the council's choice of a site for the memorial

(opposite) The memorial statue in New Westminster, British Columbia is a more "artistic" sculpture than many of the figures on Canadian monuments. Street.

necessitated the moving of the WCTU's memorial to "The Loyalist Women."[4]
This was just an example of how even the location of memorials, to say nothing
of design, had to appeal to and satisfy the diverse interests and sensitivities of
each community. There was little room for the experimental, the extraordinary, or even the new. An art historian put it another way when he said that
sculpture in Canada has suffered because it has always been at "the mercy of
public taste."[5]

Public taste, however, is an essential rather than an incidental element in
the overall historical picture of monuments. In terms of social history – the
story of ordinary people – what memorials reflect about those who commissioned them is more important than the status of the memorials as objects of
art. Still, Canadian monuments and the people who created them are far more
interesting than the amount of study devoted to them to date would indicate.
The few stories and bits of information related here serve only as an incomplete
introduction to the field.

Public taste was catered to by a wide range of artists and craftsmen. They
included the academically and formally trained, the self-taught and the delight-
fully naive. Within the limitations of the subject matter and the committee
process there has been a surprising degree of creativity and originality. Also
evident is the emergence of a clear and strong Canadian expression. Even the
mass-produced and imported sculptures that we find on many Canadian memorials are not without their artistic charm.

Some of the earliest memorials were designed abroad and the statuary
brought from overseas. Nelson's Column in Montreal had its origins in England,
while the figure for the *Monuments des Braves* at Ste-Foy, Quebec, came from
France. Original sculpture was still being imported even after the First World
War. Vernon March and other members of his family, who created the figures
for the National Memorial in Ottawa and the statue for the monument in Victoria, British Columbia, lived and worked in England. A close look at the statue
that stands in front of the Bank of Montreal's western headquarters near
Portage and Main in Winnipeg reveals that it, too, is an import. The high-laced
boots, double-breasted trench coat, and even the stylish tilt of the helmet betray
the American origins of the figure. The bank purchased the statue after it had
won a design award in New York. The sculptor, James Frazer, was also the
designer of the familiar Indian head on the U.S. nickel.

Many of the small statues that adorn monuments in such rural communities as Alameda, Saskatchewan, Thessalon, Ontario, and Tatamagouche, Nova
Scotia, have intriguing and unexpected origins. According to the *London Free
Press* of June 1, 1925 a speaker at a monument unveiling near London, Ontario,
called the new statue "a splendid example of London workmanship in Italian
marble." He was right about the marble at least. All of the Italian marble figures
were in fact carved in Carrera, Italy, probably from photographs. No two of them
are quite alike, and while they usually have a reasonable facsimile of maple leaf

The small memorial sculpture in Listowell, Ontario is one of dozens in Canada that are carved, most likely, from soft Italian marble. Shipley.

markings, the caps and details, such as piping on the sleeves, are usually more like Italian uniforms. The local monument companies acted as retailers for these statues or added them to their own designs for bases. The English firm of Walton, Goody, and Cripps, 48 Eagle Wharf Road, London, England, and Carrera, Italy, seem to have been the only ones in the business of manufacturing and distributing them.[6]

While a good many statues, both original and mass-produced, were imported for use on memorials in Canada there was a tendency towards shopping at home. Even some of the earliest monuments, including the second Brock Column (1854) and Toronto's Fenian Raid Memorial (1870), had been entirely designed and sculpted in Canada. By the end of the century there was enough demand for public monuments that it became possible for at least a few sculptors to actually make a living here.

One of the first of these was Hamilton MacCarthy (1846-1939).[7] He was the son of a noted British sculptor and had studied the art himself in England and on the Continent. MacCarthy enjoyed a reasonably successful career as a sculptor in England, primarily doing portrait busts of politicians and generals. However, in 1885, when he emigrated to Canada with his wife and six children, he planned not to work as an artist but to become a gentleman farmer. His family had interests in an estate near Toronto. Once in Canada the MacCarthys had six more children. Perhaps the need to keep moving to larger houses, along with the growing opportunities for commissions, led him back to his proven profession.

A sculptor such as MacCarthy, living and working in Victorian Canada, was very different from the picture of an artist today. He was an active member of an established church and he rode to the hounds at the Eglinton Hunt Club in Toronto. He acted Shakespearian parts in an amateur theatrical group. In 1889 he sent out an engraved invitation:

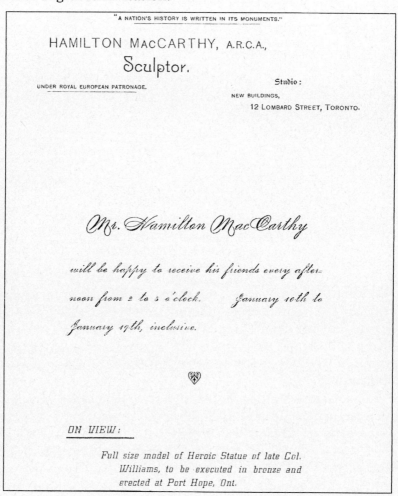

"A NATION'S HISTORY IS WRITTEN IN ITS MONUMENTS."

HAMILTON MacCARTHY, A.R.C.A.,

Sculptor.

UNDER ROYAL EUROPEAN PATRONAGE.

Studio:

NEW BUILDINGS,
12 LOMBARD STREET, TORONTO.

Mr. Hamilton MacCarthy

will be happy to receive his friends every afternoon from 2 to 5 o'clock.   January 10th to January 19th, inclusive.

ON VIEW:

Full size model of Heroic Statue of late Col.
Williams, to be executed in bronze and
erected at Port Hope, Ont.

When he later moved to Ottawa, tea was served each afternoon in his studio on the banks of the Rideau Canal. The studio had been built on the grounds of Stafford House, the family home.

Much of MacCarthy's work in Canada continued along the lines he had established in England. He helped to people Queen's Park in Toronto and Ottawa's Parliament Hill with larger-than-life bronze politicians. As well as the figure of Lieutenant-Colonel Williams, statues he designed for cities other than Ottawa and Toronto, where he lived and worked, included Boer War memorials in Halifax and Canning, Nova Scotia; Saint John, New Brunswick; Charlottetown, Prince Edward Island; Granby and Quebec City, Quebec; and Brantford, Ontario. Although he was over seventy after the First World War, MacCarthy was still active enough to contribute a few more memorial sculptures. One of these stands in Malpeque, Prince Edward Island, and another in Dundas, Ontario. Most of his sculptures are considered rather stiff by today's standards, but the Victorian men with handlebar moustaches whom they portrayed were themselves a pretty stiff lot. What MacCarthy did was not to advance into new styles and innovative forms, but to consistently and with passable skill provide people with precisely the kind of sculpture they wanted in their squares and parks.

Several other classically trained sculptors immigrated to Canada from the British Isles in the years before and after the First World War. While none of them equalled Hamilton MacCarthy in terms of the numbers of statues they produced, they were of a younger generation and their work tends to be more naturalistic and expressive.

Charles Adamson (1880-1959) attended art school in Scotland before coming to Canada, and he studied for a time in Italy under the Quebec sculptor Elzear Soucy, although it is not known if that had anything to do with his decision to come to this country. Soucy was one of the main carvers of the ornamentation on the Ottawa Parliament Buildings. While working primarily as a journalist, Adamson did execute a number of sculptural details for public buildings in Toronto and Ottawa. He completed only one memorial statue, but three versions of it were made. The original stone one was done for the Sons of England monument which stands on University Avenue in Toronto. The two copies of the soldier in winter gear were cast in bronze and found homes in Wingham and Kenora, Ontario.

Like Adamson, Frank Norbury (c.1871-1965) worked as a journalist as well as a sculptor after coming to Canada. Both Adamson and Norbury were also veterans of the First World War. Norbury wrote reviews for one of the newspapers in Edmonton, Alberta. He sculpted memorials for Holden, British Columbia, and Camrose, Alberta, but his most notable work was the statue completed for the city of Red Deer, Alberta. The figure and the base are carved from the same beautiful Manitoba Tyndall stone that was used in the Parliament

Buildings in Ottawa and other important public structures. Standing on a representation of the duck-board that lined the bottom of trenches in the First World War and supported by sand bags, the soldier on the monument looks over his shoulder in a very life-like and dynamic gesture. His trench coat hangs open, his gear is slung over his back, and his rifle looks almost too heavy for him to hold. Perhaps Major Norbury's own vivid memories of the war enabled him to capture the naturalness and humanness of a soldier's stance.

There were never a great many opportunities for sculptors to work on major pieces such as the life-sized statues for memorials. An idea of how much they wanted the chance and the difficulties involved in pursuing a commission can be seen from Frank Norbury's negotiations with the memorial committee in Red Deer.[8] First of all he had to make many trips from his home in Edmonton to Red Deer at his own expense. In May 1921, after a local monument dealer had been awarded the contract for the memorial, Norbury was among the people in Edmonton who were consulted about ideas for a suitable statue. He was allowed to submit a model himself, but it was on the understanding that the one hundred dollar cost would be applied against the final contract price should he be asked to do the work. He was given the job, and in June of 1921 he was back asking the committee for an advance of five hundred dollars to help cover the cost of the stone that he had already ordered at his own expense. It was four months before he received the money. The work took Norbury the better part of a year to complete. Considering that all his expenses including delivery came out of the five thousand and fifty dollars he was paid, it is clear that his earnings were modest.

Alfred Howell (b. 1889), who had the contentious dealings with the memorial committee in Saint John, New Brunswick, was another Englishman who studied art in his home country before coming to Canada. He taught at Toronto's Central Technical School after arriving in the city in 1913. His designs for memorial sculpture won competitions in Oshawa, Pembroke, Guelph, and Sault Ste. Marie, Ontario, as well as in Saint John. Howell's monuments were often more complex than earlier ones found in Canada. They were also highly symbolic. The one in Sault Ste. Marie shows a female figure, probably representing victory or peace, treading on a male figure who symbolizes war. There are two bronze relief plaques attached to stones on either side of the monument; one, portrays the men of the city reluctantly going to war and the other, shows them returning, wounded, tired, and bearing their dead. Howell's designs seem fairly traditional to modern eyes, but they were considerably more romantic in concept than the static figures of the previous century. Howell claimed, for instance, that the inspiration for the monument in Guelph, Ontario, came to him in a dream. He had already designed a pylon with a soldier on it, but in his vision he saw a spirit in the form of a female figure rising behind the boy in uniform.[9]

Of the sculptors who came to Canada from the British Isles, Howell was the only one who did not make his permanent home here. He moved to Cleveland, Ohio, in the 1950s. Another graduate of a Scottish art academy, J. Massey Rhind (1860-1936), moved in the opposite direction. He had immigrated to New York in the late 1800s, but as success there brought him an increasing degree of affluence, if not great wealth, he spent much of his time at his summer home in Chester, Nova Scotia. "It's a pretty lively place in the summer-time," Rhind is reported to have said, "but I imagine it's as dead as a mackerel in the winter."[10] Massey Rhind's slightly condescending attitude towards Nova Scotia came out as well in two conflicting stories about how he came to donate a memorial statue to the town of Chester. He claimed that the whole thing was his idea and that he had helped out the poor misguided locals. But one of those locals said in his memoirs that the committee knew exactly what they wanted and approached Rhind to get it.[11] Rhind's connection with Nova Scotia, however, led not only to his giving a statue to Chester but to commissions for works in Halifax and New Glasgow.

Massey Rhind was not the most original of artists, as one can see from comparing his "City of Halifax" figure with the Italian Renaissance sculptor Donatello's statue of St. George. He was, however, a stickler for detail. He once rummaged through a museum in Philadelphia until he found some old clothes that had belonged to a former city father: he was sculpting a figure of the man and wanted to get the proportions exact. When he did the statue of the High-lander for Chester, nothing would do but that a man in uniform serve as a model. Russel Zinck, who had gone to medical school at McGill in Montreal after his war service, was the Chester native who made the eventful trip to New York. Zinck later practised medicine in nearby Lunenburg, Nova Scotia, and even in his eighties his sturdy features were still recognizable in Rhind's statue.

As well as trained sculptors, a number of stonecutters originally from Britain worked on some of the more humble memorials in Canada. One of these was a man named William Loveday, who settled in London, Ontario. Some of Loveday's recollections suggest the interest and care that people showed towards monument building in the years after the First World War. In a competition for the contract to erect a memorial cross in London, his bid was higher than the others because he proposed that his craftsmen take extra time for a finer finish. One of the committee members came to ask Loveday if there was really any difference. He simply had the man touch one piece of stone, then another, with a finer surface. Loveday was awarded the contract. On another occasion he was helping to erect a plain stone obelisk in the village of Wheatley, Ontario. The work of raising the monument was very tricky and soon a crowd, the whole community in fact, came to watch. When the stone finally slipped into place there were wild cheers and congratulations from the enthusiastic crowd.

Dr. Russel Zinck, pictured here when he was in his eighties, had just returned from service overseas during World War I when he posed in uniform for sculptor J. Massey Rhind. The resulting statue is the monument in Chester, Nova Scotia. Street.

Not all the immigrant craftsmen who worked on memorials were from Britain. Two that are remembered in widely different areas in western Canada were in fact Germans. A man named Hensrude was responsible for the stone masonry on several memorials in southwestern Saskatchewan, while another mason named Schmidt built the cairn in Osoyoos, British Columbia. While the names recorded on the monuments endure, most of the craftsmen who built them have, unfortunately, been forgotten.

The two most notable American sculptors who immigrated to Canada were women. Frances Loring received most of her training in Europe before returning to the United States and meeting Florence Wyle at the art school where she was studying in Chicago. The two first worked in New York together but around 1908 moved to Toronto, where they spent the rest of their lives. In 1968 they died within a few months of one another. Frances Loring's work include war memorials in Galt, Ontario, at Osgoode Hall in Toronto, and in St. Stephen, New Brunswick. Florence Wyle sculpted the bronze plaque commemorating Edith Cavell which stands at the corner of College Street and University Avenue in Toronto. Both of them did small statues depicting women at work during the First World War.

While the artists and craftsmen that have been discussed above came originally from outside Canada, the majority of those who created memorials in this country were either born here or came as very young children and spent their working lives in this country. Some were essentially self-taught, some studied here, and others honed their skills at foreign academies; but together they can be said to represent a respectable native-Canadian tradition.

Inspired by the many fine examples of French Canadian church sculpture he grew up with, as well as the natural forms he found around him in his rural home at Ste-Sophie d'Halifax, Quebec, Louis-Philippe Hébert (1850-1917) started whittling wood at an early age. Then, when he was nineteen, he joined the Zouaves and went to Italy to fight for the Pope. The sight of the ancient sculptural treasures in Rome further excited the young Hébert. Back in Quebec he continued to work on his own until his growing skill came to the attention of the painter Napoleon Bourassa, father of the great Quebec journalist and politician, Henri. With some additional instruction in Bourassa's studio Hébert was able to launch himself into a successful career as a sculptor. The statue of Colonel de Salaberry at Chambly, Quebec, finished in 1881, was one of Hebert's early works. One of his crowning achievements came many years later with the completion of the Boer War Memorial for Calgary. Unveiled in 1914, it remains the only Canadian-designed statue of a horse and mounted rider.[12]

Emile Brunet (b. 1899) was another Quebec-born sculptor who was primarily self-taught. He worked for his father in the family stonecutting firm and is said to have carved the statue of "The Patriot" for the monument at St. Denis, Quebec, when he was only fourteen years old. Subsequently, he won a scholarship to study art in Chicago. There he was offered further scholarships if he would become an American citizen, but Brunet wanted to remain a Canadian and so he returned to work in Montreal. The animated soldier on the memorial in Longueuil, Quebec, is another of his works.

The West, too, produced an interesting sculptor, who seems to have learned his craft by his own wits. Little is known about Nicolas Pirotton, but he worked in St. Boniface, Manitoba, and his memorial statues dot the eastern prairies. The face of a soldier on the keystone of the memorial arch at St. Andrews, Manitoba, was probably one of his early works. It has a very naive but quite lively character. A similar but somewhat more developed figure appears on the memorial in Morden, Manitoba. A portrait bust of the French general, Ferdinand Foch, was sculpted by Pirotton for the monument in St. Claude, Manitoba. Pirotton's pensive soldier in a trench coat shows up in several places, including Weyburn, Saskatchewan, and MacGregor, Manitoba. It was even copied by a firm in Ontario for the memorial in Gananoque, on the St. Lawrence River. The same figure is found in company with a statue of Joan of Arc on the memorial in St. Pierre, Manitoba. If it is true, as proposed, that Pirotton had little or no formal training in sculpture, then the St. Pierre monument is all the more remarkable in both conception and execution.

Although his background was very different from most other Canadian sculptors, R. Tait McKenzie (1867-1938) can also be counted among the artists who learned their craft on their own. McKenzie was born in Almonte, Ontario, near Ottawa. He studied medicine at McGill University, where he aquired his fascination for anatomy. This life-long interest led him into a career as a leading expert on physical fitness and explained his skill in sculpting the human form. Much of his professional medical life was spent in the United States, but he served with the British Army during the First World War and as inspector of convalescent hospitals in Canada after 1918. When he retired, he refurbished an old mill outside Almonte as a studio and home. As well as the monument for his home town, he did several smaller memorial sculptures, such as the statue of Captain Guy Drummond of the Black Watch, which is now in the Public Archives in Ottawa, and of Lieutenant-Colonel George Harold Baker, which stands in the lobby of the Canadian House of Commons.[13] He also did several memorial statues for American and British institutions and communities, and the Scottish-American Monument (1927) that was erected in Edinburgh, Scotland. It was dedicated to all the North Americans of Scots descent who fell in the Great War.

Walter Allward (1876-1955) was probably the most successful of the self-taught Canadian sculptors, both in terms of recognition and artistic accomplishment. His parents came from Newfoundland and he was born and raised in Toronto. As a young man he went to work in an architect's office, and from there his aptitude in design and drawing developed into a passion for sculpture. One of Allward's earliest commissions was the statue for the memorial in Toronto's Queen's Park dedicated to those who fought in the North-West Rebellion. That statue was done in the last years of the past century and was followed in the first decade of the new era by monuments in the same city that commemorated the War of 1812 and the Boer War.

All of these early works by Allward were sculpted in a naturalistic and classical style. The detail of the uniforms and equipment of the soldiers on the Toronto Boer War Memorial, their facial expressions, and their striding posture are completely lifelike. In the dramatic flight of the winged angel that tops that memorial, however, Allward began to play with the style that was to characterize his later statues, such as the monuments for Stratford and Peterborough, Ontario. They are more impressionistic than realistic and are also quite theatrical in their symbolism. Each consists of two male figures clothed not in carefully detailed uniforms, but only in swirls of drapery. They represent the heroic spirit turning back the wraith of barbarism. The same kind of dynamic energy and tension that filled August Rodin's work is evident in Walter Allward's sculpture, although it is not clear if the French master had any direct influence on Allward's ideas.

Allward was chosen to design Canada's memorial on Vimy Ridge in France. The monument took him ten years to complete and was dedicated in 1936. The figures there are in the same strong style as those of his later work in Canada. It is perhaps a tribute to the beauty and power of his work that during several years of Nazi occupation in France, Allward's Vimy Ridge Monument was never touched. "Splendid native sculpture," the Bobcaygeon *Independent* called his work in the December 2, 1920 issue. The appreciative small-town paper went on to say that "Ontario has reason to be proud of the art of one of its native sculptors."

Similar praise had been accorded another native artist some years earlier. Referring to Montreal's Boer War Memorial in 1907, the May 31 *Times* of Richmond, Quebec, said, "The monument itself may be considered a Canadian glory, not only on account of the idea it symbolizes, but because it is the product of Canadian genius." The genius in question belonged to George Hill (1862-1934). Like his fellow Quebecer, Emile Brunet, Hill had grown up in the province's stone-working business. He apprenticed with his father in the granite quarries of the Stanstead region of the Eastern Townships. Hill, however, went to Paris at a fairly early age and received a complete classical education in sculpture. Some of Hill's monuments, including the figures in Montreal West, Richmond, and Lachute, Quebec, at Harbord Collegiate in Toronto, and Morrisburg, Ontario, consist of single statues, but he was also one of the first sculptors in Canada to construct group statues. The three soldiers on the monument in Sherbrooke, Quebec, are similar to the trio in Charlottetown, Prince Edward Island. The angel on the top of the same Sherbrooke monument shows up again

The cenotaph in Charlottetown, Prince Edward Island is the work of Montreal sculptor George Hill. Shipley.

in Westmount, Quebec. These were pretty grandiose efforts, and like most Canadian sculptors of the time Hill had to have the actual casting of the bronzes done overseas. He set up a studio in Brussels, near the foundry that undertook much of his work. It was there that he was photographed standing beside the angel, soldier, and boy scout figures he had designed for the memorial in Pictou, Nova Scotia. The necessity of travelling often to Europe to supervise the casting of statues meant that artists such as Hill used up much of their commission on expenses and sometimes missed competitions for other memorials while they were away.

By the early 1920s what had been the William A. Rogers Company, Foundry Division, in Toronto, had been taken over by the hard-working sales-men and sculptors of the Tickell family. Their promotional booklet indicated that at least some of the monumental sculpture in the country was then being made here. "A splendid Canadian achievement," the brochure said, and it went on to point out that Tickell's was "the only Bronze Foundry in Canada that . . . successfully attempted large statuary castings."[14] The statue in the picture was a copy of the pensive soldier figure created by Nicolas Pirotton.

Two of the three best-known sculptors in the next generation were sons of the earlier masters, Hamilton MacCarthy and Louis-Philippe Hébert. The third was a student of Allward's. Coeur de Lion MacCarthy came to Canada with his family in 1885 as a young child. He is said to have been the model for his father's Boer War statue which now stands behind the National Arts Centre in Ottawa. Whether or not that is true he was certainly influenced in his choice of career by his father, and after starting his training at home he went to study in the Paris art academies. The younger MacCarthy's exuberant and emotional stat-ues have a good deal more life than his father's, but are still fairly conventional. Typical of his style are the statues of the rifle-and-helmet-waving celebrants on memorials in Verdun, Quebec, and Goderich, Ontario. Probably the works he is best known for are the three identical statues done as memorials for former CPR employees. One of these is in the old Windsor Station in Montreal. An-other stands in front of the CPR station in Winnipeg and the third is at the harbour-front station in Vancouver.

Henri Hébert (1884-1950), unlike his father Louis-Philippe, had the advan-tage of exposure to the best teachers both in Montreal and Paris from a very early age. He enjoyed several periods of study in Europe in fact, before being appointed to a teaching position at McGill University in 1909. The First World War had a deep affect on Hébert's sensitivities and the two war monuments that he did are quite different from other contemporary sculpture. For the Out-remont section of Montreal he created a memorial which shows the mourning city represented by a graceful female form. In Yarmouth, Nova Scotia, Hébert's soldier looks as though he has just marched out of the trenches. The realistic, mud-splattered figure wears a leather vest and leg wrappings over his puttees;

his rifle is covered with canvas to keep the water off. No other statue in the country captures the look of a war-weary soldier so well. It is not known whether Hébert actually used a photograph as his inspiration, but the Yarmouth statue bears a surprising resemblance to a famous picture of a soldier that is now in the collection of the National War Museum.

Emmanual Hahn (1881-1957) was another child immigrant. He arrived in Canada with his family in 1888 at the age of seven. His father was a geologist and began to travel extensively in the north. From his youth and throughout his life Mani, as he was called, had the same love for the Canadian wilderness that his father had acquired during his expeditions. Hahn studied sculpture under the direction of Walter Allward in Toronto and completed his education in the years before the First World War at the Stuttgart Kunstakademie in Germany. Through his work for the Thompson Monument Company, which was probably the leading producer of monuments in Canada, Hahn may have designed more memorials than any other individual in the country. About twenty statues and several other cenotaphs are known or thought to be his work. Some of these are duplicates or even multiple copies of the same design, yet each is a technically accomplished piece and each had an appeal to the people who chose it. Hahn must have lost friends on both sides in the war: the faces on his statues in Moncton, New Brunswick, and Killarney, Manitoba, are those of mourning and loss.

Emmanual Hahn taught at the Ontario College of Art for many years, and among his students were some who eventually went on to sculpt memorials on their own. One of them was Hames Saull, who designed the Oak Bay Memorial in Victoria, British Columbia. Another was Elizabeth Wyn Wood, who did the monument for Welland, Ontario. Wyn Wood also became Hahn's wife and there are some hints of their influence on each other's work. Hahn's unsuccessful entry in a competition for a memorial to Lord Selkirk had a long sloping base. The same base showed up in Wyn Wood's submission for the memorial in Winnipeg. That monument, as we know, was never built, but the base finally appeared in the Welland memorial. We do not know whose idea it was originally.

A few other artists are known to have sculpted one or two monuments each. Often these were for their home towns or for places close to home. A Major Patterson designed the statue of a wounded soldier for the memorial in New Westminster, British Columbia. The actual sculpting was done by A. Fabri.[15] R.G. Heughan of Montreal is supposed to have designed the cenotaph for Regina, but the sculpture that was part of it looked so much like George Clemeshaw's St. Julien Monument in Belgium that there were inevitable charges of plagiarism. Clemeshaw was a Regina native. Mrs. Hilliard Taylor of Winnipeg did the Next-of-Kin Monument that stands by the parliament buildings in that city, as well as the statue for Prince Albert, Saskatchewan. Another Winnipegger, Hubert Garnier, created the Belgian Memorial for St. Boniface.

Jim Watson sits in his New Glasgow, Nova Scotia home. On the table in front of him is a picture of Jim working on the Trenton, Nova Scotia memorial and the finished sculpture. Street.

The hands of naive or untrained sculptors can be seen in monuments at St. Andrews Manitoba (left) and Dorchester, New Brunswick (right). Street.

Ivor Lewis was a T. Eaton Company executive in Toronto. He did the small, winter-garbed soldier statue that serves as the memorial for Burlington, Ontario. Alvin Hilts studied sculpture with Frances Loring and Florence Wyle in Toronto, and he designed the female figure on the memorial in his home town of Newmarket, Ontario. James Watson won a scholarship to attend the Royal Academy in England while he was studying at the Nova Scotia College of Art in the 1930s. After returning home to Trenton, Nova Scotia, Watson went to work in the pattern shop of the local rolling-stock plant. There, instead of sculptures, he cast railway car components. But he did work part-time with a nearby New Glasgow, Nova Scotia, monument firm. That led to his carving statues for his home town of Trenton and for Judique, on Cape Breton Island.

The creators of many memorials and memorial statues in Canada are simply not known. Some relatively unsophisticated statues can be found in the Maritimes in places such as Woodstock, Grand Falls, and Dorchester, New Brunswick, and it could be that they all came from the granite quarries of H. McGratton and Sons in St. George, New Brunswick. In southeastern Ontario there are concrete monuments at Campbellford and Roseneath that may have been built by the same contractor, A. H. McKeel and Sons, who erected a similar memorial at Trent River. On Prince Edward Island, in the Bruce Peninsula, and Algoma area of Ontario, in the vicinity of Leduc, Alberta, and in other regions, there are clusters of distinct memorials that no doubt owe their origins to now-forgotten local craftsmen.

EIGHT
Cenotaph – The Empty Tomb

and he spent a long time watching
from a lonely wooden tower.
Leonard Cohen: "Suzanne Takes You Down"

When an artist paints a portrait there are really two pictures. One is of the
subject and the other is of the painter.[1] The same is true of public monuments.
When a community gets together and raises a statue or cairn, the memorial has
the significance the builders intended, but it also has the potential to convey
information about the builders themselves. Where there are distinct patterns
in public monuments – symbols that are seen over and over again in different
places – then there may even be a picture of the very nature of the society in
which they are found. Certain patterns in Canadian monuments prevail from
coast to coast like the northwest wind.

Had memorials been erected by governments, we could have interpreted
them as propaganda. In totalitarian regimes, for instance, monuments are com-
monly used to convince the people that a war was justified and that it resulted
in a glorious victory. Had memorials been erected at the fancy of particular
individuals, they would not be as interesting. A prominent Toronto citizen donated statues of King Edward VII and Winston Churchill to the city.[2] They are
very impressive and they tell us of the donor's fascination with monument
sculpture, but they indicate nothing about popular sentiments. Had monuments been erected primarily by a specific group, accounting for them would
have been of more limited significance. In the past twenty years local branches
of the Royal Canadian Legion have continued to build memorials in towns that
did not already have them, such as Bradford, Ontario, and Port Moody, British
Columbia. But these are generally located beside Legion halls, and they are
quite different in character from the older memorials that dominate the parks

(opposite) An altar of sacrifice is suggested by this monument in the cemetary at Fernie, British
Columbia. Shipley.

and main streets of so many Canadian communities and were the result of broader movements. Finally, if the styles of monuments had been primarily the personal expression of artists the way most modern sculpture is, then deciphering the artists' intention would have been the key to understanding.

The designs, locations, and even the original decisions to build monuments in Canada were not determined by governments, individuals, special groups, or particular artists. Rather, they were matters of community consensus. The resulting memorials are, therefore, quite clearly expressions of popular feelings. The full meaning of the feelings are less obvious. The values and ideas that people hold most deeply are not always stated explicitly. In fact, it almost seems that the stronger and more emotional an issue is, the greater the tendency to deal with it in some unspoken way. Ceremonies and symbols can best be understood when seen as expressions of otherwise unspoken social sentiments.[3] Remembrance Day is not the least important of the ceremonial observances on our national calendar, and since the Armistice ritual centres on the monument, it helps to consider ceremony and symbol together.

They are both essentially religious. Religion undertakes, in part, to answer the most troubling questions that plague our spirits. On November 11 (July 1 in Newfoundland) the question at hand concerns the thousands and thousands of people who have been killed in wars. Was there any purpose or meaning to the suffering and death of so many? The answer that is offered is symbolic and its explicit meaning is offered in only a whisper.

The ritualized answer must be seen in the context of a society whose principle deity is a man who suffered and was, brutally and seemingly without reason, killed. Christian teaching, however, tells us that Christ did not die. Because He sacrificed Himself in the service of others He triumphed over death, was resurrected, and won eternal life. In the Apostles' Creed the faithful repeat, "I believe in the resurrection of the body and the life everlasting." This is one of the central articles of faith in the Christian doctrine. The Eucharist or Holy Communion symbolizes and reinforces this belief.

Like Christ and the Christian martyrs our soldiers died violent deaths. The Remembrance Day ceremony, like the Eucharist, attempts to account satisfactorily for their passing. At a critical point in the service the bugle sounds "The Last Post." That is the traditional end to the soldier's day. The Last Post symbolizes death and is followed by two minutes of silence. The silence is usually timed to coincide with the eleventh hour of the eleventh day of the eleventh month. That was the moment the First Great War ended in 1918. During the silence we reflect on the dead and mourn their passing. Their suffering in war is reminiscent of the martyrs' torment and of Christ's descent into hell. At the end of the two minutes, "Reveille" is sounded. That bugle call begins the day. What is symbolized by Reveille is an awakening and in fact a resurrection. The soldiers, by their sacrifice, are identified with a martyrdom that wins them eternal life. A hymn that is often sung as part of this service says:

Faith of our fathers, living still,
In spite of dungeon, fire and sword.

The form of the monuments themselves pick up the symbolism where the Remembrance Day ceremony leaves off. "Cenotaph" is a term that has usually been applied, in Canada, to a specific style of memorial: a plain stone pylon without statuary. In fact, any memorial that does not mark a grave could be called a cenotaph. The word is derived from two Greek roots whose meanings are "empty" and "tomb." A cenotaph can be seen symbolically as an "empty tomb" in two different ways: it does not contain the actual physical remains of those it commemorates the way a real tomb does, but rather represents the resting place of soldiers who are buried far away and sailors lost at sea. And a cenotaph is an "empty tomb" in the same sense that Christ's grave was empty: because of the resurrection.

Descriptions of monuments given at the time of building serve to reinforce the religious character of their symbolism. A booklet that survives from the day the memorial cross in Mahone Bay, Nova Scotia, was dedicated is an example. It tells us that the roughly-hewn base of the cross is there to remind us of the rough and hardy nature of Nova Scotia's sons, while the polished stone of remembrance above the base reminds us of the refining process of God's Providence. It says that the fallible human spirit was fashioned into heroism amid the fires of war and its inspiration was Christ's sacrifice.[4]

The cenotaph in Whitby, Ontario, was described even more completely in Oshawa's *Ontario Reformer* of June 5, 1924:

> The composition of the memorial is in three, namely, base, die and crown. This is in keeping with the great Three In One by whose aid we have been able to overcome our trials. The die has on each side three steps with the shadow of the cross on the top step. Below the honour roll is the Latin word *Resurgent* (they shall live again) showing our faith in the new life, and the Resurrection. Surmounting the whole is the crown piece in the form of a Roman altar of sacrifice . . . the altar of Canadian honour and high spirit which, although we passed through deep valleys and sorrow and sacrifice, still remains burning as a symbol in the whole world of our undying faith and integrity.

The tripartite feature is often seen in monuments, including ones found at Flesherton, Ontario, Calgary, Alberta, and Summerland, British Columbia.

More convincing than surviving written references to religious symbolism in memorials are the visual symbols that were included in their designs, consciously or unconsciously in compliance with tradition. A preponderance of these visual symbols carry the same hopeful message of resurrection. Chief among them is the poppy. Small artificial poppies are sold by the Canadian Legion in November and worn by millions. They are present in the permanent stone and bronze of monuments as well. Poppies are carved on the flag-draped stone altar in the veterans' plot of the mountainside cemetery in Fernie, British Columbia. They wind around the small cross on the main street of Shubenacadie, Nova Scotia. Even in the impressionistic sculpture at Stratford, Ontario, stylized poppies emerge from the cast metal. On dozens of the simplest memorial cairns the heads of the bolts that hold the plaques are shaped like tiny poppies.

The poppy is a symbol of remembrance in many countries. It was officially adopted in Canada in 1921 at the urging of a Frenchwoman, Mme. E. Guerin, who was travelling around the world to promote the idea. At least a hundred years earlier a newspaper correspondent had noted how thickly poppies grew around the graves of the dead from the Napoleonic Wars, but after the First World War the poppy owed much of its currency to a thirteen-line verse that had been scribbled on a scrap of paper by an exhausted Canadian doctor in 1915. In the midst of the bloody fighting at Ypres, Lieutenant-Colonel John McCrae, from Guelph, Ontario, wrote the poem that begins, "In Flanders fields the poppies blow." It was published in *Punch* before the end of the war and it immediately caught people's imaginations. The image touched a deep chord. In Christian art the blood-red flower had long been connected with Christ's passion. More important even than that was the observable reality in northern Europe. McCrae and others could not help noticing that the poppy was the first thing to grow on disturbed ground. On roadsides where ditches had been dug, at the edges of plowed fields, and most of all on the tortured no man's land of the Great War battlefields, the poppy was the first life to appear from previous destruction. It was the most natural symbol of rebirth, of resurrection.

A number of other floral motifs are frequently found in the designs of Canadian memorials. A palm frond is carved on the base of an obelisk in Humbolt, Saskatchewan. A wreath is held by an angel figure in Georgetown, Ontario. A laurel branch is draped across a dead soldier's discarded gear on the memorial in Fredericton, New Brunswick. The palm, wreath, and laurel are very ancient symbols that predate the Christian era.[5] They were offered as signs of victory to Greek athletes and Roman generals. Palm fronds were strewn in front of Christ during his entry into Jerusalem in the event that is celebrated annually in the church calendar as Palm Sunday. As with many other ancient symbols, however, these victory or triumphal offerings took on a new meaning in Christian iconography. It is not victory in the realm of earthly affairs that is celebrated, but the triumph of life over death. When the motifs appear on Canadian memorials they are not meant to be indicative of victory in the war; rather, they speak of the eternal life that is the hope of the faithful and that alone can make sense of the loss of so many people.

One of the best-loved monument forms in Canada is the mourning soldier such as this statue in Springhill, Nova Scotia. The poppies at the foot of the cross are among the Christian symbols that are common on such statues. Street.

Along with the symbols of triumph there are also a number of memorial statues that display gestures of great exuberance. The soldiers on monuments in Liverpool, Nova Scotia, Verdun, Quebec, Goderich, Ontario, and Winnipeg, Manitoba, hold either their rifles or helmets aloft. Sometimes they are described as cheering at the news of victory. A statue of this kind in Kingston, Ontario, however, indicates that another sentiment may be intended by the gestures. On the base of the Kingston figure there is a carved cross with poppies wound around it. From behind the cross radiate the shafts of morning sunlight. Once again the cumulative image is one of resurrection and triumph, not over an enemy, but over death itself.

The identification of our soldiers with Christian martyrs is further emphasized by those statues that portray fallen soldiers in the traditional poses of the saints. This is evident when we compare the statues in Chatham and Shelbourne, Ontario, with the Renaissance statue of St. Longinus by the master Bernini which is found in St. Peter's in Rome. Here again is the expansive, triumphant gesture of one who has seen a vision. Even from the depths of despair the figure seems to be beholding a great truth. St. Longinus, too, was a soldier; he holds the spear with which he is supposed to have pierced the side of Christ while our soldiers hold the rifles and bayonets with which they killed their fellow men.

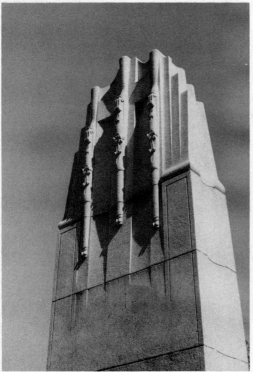

(left) The three rifles on the cenotaph in Thunder Bay - Port Arthur form a soldier's Calvary. Shipley.

(right) The 21st Battalion monument in Kingston, Ontario shows a soldier seeing a heavenly vision rather than cheering an earthly victory. Shipley.

One of the most common memorial figures in Canada is a soldier holding a rifle and standing with downcast eyes beside a cross of the kind used to mark temporary graves near the battlefields of the western front. We find him in various forms in Springhill, Nova Scotia; Gaspé, Quebec; Hanover, Cornwall, Port Dalhousie, and North Bay, Ontario; Killarney, Manitoba; and Fernie, British Columbia. That is only the beginning of the list. The same posture, with its symbolic trappings, is the usual way of representing the saints. From the sculpted figures that line the entrances to Gothic cathedrals, through Donatello's Renaissance statue of St. George, and in the paintings of various periods, saints are pictured in the same way. They each hold one or more objects that identify them or are connected with their martyrdom. St. George, for example, holds the lance and sword of a knight. The words to another of the hymns sung at Remembrance Day ceremonies say:

> O valiant hearts who to your glory came,
> Through dust and conflict and through battles flame,
> Tranquil you lie, your knightly virtue proved.

St. Catherine of Messina is usually represented with the spiked wheel on which she was killed. St. Peter, the keeper of the gates of Heaven, holds a key, while St. Lawrence, who was martyred by being roasted alive, holds a small grille.

These symbols do not belong solely to church icons nor are they understood only by art experts. The Canadian warship, *St. Laurent,* has the grille as its emblem. St. Andrew, the patron saint of the Scots, is traditionally represented holding the X-shaped cross on which he was said to have been crucified; that image is found not only in Church paintings but also on the cap and collar badges worn by thousands of Canadian soldiers in Scottish regiments. In much the same way as St. Andrew, the soldier figure on so many memorials in the country, holds his rifle and the Flanders grave-marker as the symbols of his martyrdom.

In the *Northern Advance* of June 29, 1922, published at the time of the memorial unveiling in Barrie, Ontario, this type of figure was described as mourning the loss of his comrade before leaving for home. However, that is an explanation that would better describe a slightly different pose that is found in the monuments at Lethbridge, Alberta, and Regina, Saskatchewan. In those places the statue stands in the position known in the military drill manual as "resting on arms reversed." It is the vigil pose taken by four servicemen at the corners of a coffin during a military funeral and at the four corners of a cenotaph during a Remembrance service.

Artists have also portrayed the Christian hero at the moment of his ascension. Giotto, for instance, painted St. Anthony being lifted out of the Italian countryside as if flying to Paradise. The idea of ascension is current outside Christianity as well. Mohammed ascended into Heaven from the site of the

Dome of the Rock in Jerusalem. The Valkyries, who were the daughters of the chief Norse god Odin – not to be confused with the Daughters of the Empire – were supposed to swoop down on fiery steeds and carry fallen warriors from the battlefield to Valhalla. The CPR memorial statues that stand inside or in front of the railway stations in Vancouver, Winnipeg, and Montreal depict an angel carrying a dead Canadian soldier skyward. The figure of the soldier in Guelph, Ontario, also seems to be ascending with the help of an angel. On the back of the brick memorial in Streetsville, Ontario, there is a bronze plaque that shows a soldier suspended in the air and seeming to move towards the image of Christ above him.

The association of the soldier's death with Christian martyrdom led inexorably to identification of the soldier with Christ himself. Numerous examples in literature and the graphic arts hint at this. During the war the English poet Wilfred Owen wrote to a friend: "For 14 hours yesterday I was at work, teaching Christ how to lift his cross by numbers and how to adjust his crown and not imagine he'd thirst till after the last halt. I attended his supper to see that there were not complaints and inspected his feet that they should be worthy of the nails. I see to it that he's dumb and stands at attention before his accusers. With pieces of silver I buy him every day and with maps I make him familiar with the topography of Golgotha."[6]

(opposite) In the Montreal suburb of Jacques Cartier a soldier is portrayed in death but ascending into the realm beyong. Street.

(right) This small sculpture that is not actually a war memorial depicts "Canada's Golgotha." Shipley.

A story circulated during the war that German soldiers had actually executed Canadian prisoners by crucifying them within sight of their own lines. It may have had its origins in the not uncommon sight of men "hanging on the old barbed wire," as the words of a popular song put it, but the story suited the propaganda of the time and it persisted. A small, one-metre high sculpture by the British artist F.W. Wood depicts this grisly scene. The sculpture, called "Canada's Golgotha," is now in the Beaverbrook Memorial Art Collection in Ottawa. Whether or not the incident ever took place is not as important as the fact that people were struck by its symbolism. After the war the idea filtered down through the collective consciousness. A full-page picture appeared in the Ottawa *Citizen* in 1928 showing a dead Canadian soldier at the foot of a crucified Christ. The memorial inscription in the Manitoba village of Douglas reads in part:

> They died unnoticed in the muddy trench,
> Nay! God was with them, and they did not blench,
> Filled them with holy fires that naught could quench
> And when he saw their work on earth was done
> He gently called to them
>   My sons, my sons.

When the cenotaph in Guelph, Ontario, was unveiled on July 4, 1927, the *Daily Mercury* told of one speaker who had talked of "a heroism springing from unflinching self-sacrifice such as mankind has only seen once before – in the Cross of Calvary."

As the Great War dragged on, the casualty lists grew more and more appalling. The struggle seemed to continue without any apparent movement or sense of progress towards an end. People came to think of the war not so much as fighting but as sacrificing. It seemed that victory would belong not to the side that was strongest, bravest, or most resourceful in tactics and strategy, but to the side that had the most people willing to die for it. A recruiting poster in Windsor, Ontario, reminded people that Lord Kitchener had said, "The War will last three years and will be won by the last Million Men."[7] The poster went on to say, "The third year has commenced – Join to-day." The year came and went and thousands more Canadians enlisted, but not even that was enough. Like Christ, in the analogy of Wilfred Owen's letter, the volunteers had to learn to stand dumb before their accusers.

Like many Christian concepts the idea of sacrifice had Judaic and even pagan antecedents. The ritual slaughter of animals had a long history. It was an act of unquestioning obedience performed in order to appease all-powerful gods. When plague carried off the first-born of Egypt the houses of the Jews were passed over because their doors were marked with the blood of sacrificed lambs.

Christ made himself the Pascal Lamb, and we are passed over by death because of his sacrifice. In ancient times the animals that were offered to the gods were burned on altars. These were sometimes makeshift piles of stone and sometimes more formal cut-stone arrangements. Many memorials in Canada take the form of cairns or stone altars that are like the ancient ones, and some are further decorated with symbolic flames. The crown piece of the Whitby, Ontario, monument was described as a Roman altar and there are stone flames atop memorials in Montmagny, Quebec, and in Carlton Place and Espanola, Ontario. In Dryden, Ontario, the memorial has symbolic flames made from neon tubing that actually flicker.

The theme of sacrifice and crucifixion is carried through in many other forms of memorials. In Watford, Ontario, there is a cross carved on the front of the monument. It is flanked by two swords which, besides being military symbols, are themselves crosses. Together the three form an image of Calvary. In the Port Arthur section of Thunder Bay, Ontario, this Calvary motif is repeated with an interesting modern flavour. When soldiers were hurriedly buried on the Western Front at times when no grave markers were readily available, the graves were designated by sticking the man's rifle, muzzle first, into the ground. Sometimes the helmet was placed on top of the butt. When we look closely at the Port Arthur memorial we see three rifles, muzzles down, with a cross hinted at in the stone work. This is a true soldier's Calvary.

The former town of Preston, Ontario, is now part of the amalgamated city of Cambridge. In the Preston memorial the identification of a soldier's death with crucifixion reached a particular degree of clarity. There a statue of a soldier stands with his arms outstretched in an unmistakable cruciform position.

The religious nature of Canadian memorials is often emphasized by the positioning of the monument. In many cultures, towns and cities have centred around physical symbols that have to do with expressions of nationalism, identity, and local pride. The great boulevards of Paris radiate out from Arc de Triomphe, and Athens rings the ancient fortress of the Acropolis. In a similar way there has often been an object such as a statue or a structure such as a church or temple that serves as a spiritual focus for the community. Sometimes they are one and the same. The cathedrals were both the physical and spiritual centres of medieval European cities. In Quebec and other mainly Catholic areas of the country there is often a religious statue outside the single parish church. Because most of the rest of Canada has been predominantly Protestant, however, there were always several churches in each place and no one obvious spiritual centre. The levelling effect and pervasive experience of the war gave communities of mixed faith the opportunity and inclination to come together and create for themselves one common devotional site. The Remembrance Day service has been the main and perhaps the only inter-denominational observance in Canadian towns. It usually includes not only representatives from all the

The cenotaph in Preston, part of Cambridge, Ontario, is a quintessencial Canadian memorial. The original central monument was built after World War I with the side stones added after 1945. The carved figure in an artillery man's cape is similar to, if not copied from, an English statue. He stands as "a wall of defence" but also in the position of one crucified. Both young people and veterans are present at the service pictured. Bernd Krueger.

Christian sects, but Jews and members of other faiths as well. Only a thing that was both spiritually significant and acceptable to an entire community could occupy the symbolic centre of our communities in the way that cenotaphs do.

There are places in the country where the old custom of religious statuary and the practice of centrally located memorials celebrating major historical events come together. In Trinity Bay, Newfoundland, a predominantly Anglican town, the cenotaph is located in the churchyard. In the Catholic fishing town of Caraquet, New Brunswick, the soldiers' memorial is also found in the grounds of the parish church. In Cheticamp, Cape Breton Island, a statue of Christ shares the space in front of the church with the cenotaph.

There are some places where the memorial and the religious statue are one and the same. In Placentia, Newfoundland, a pure white figure of Christ of the Sacred Heart stands in the square in front of the church. On its base are inscribed the names of local men killed in the war. In Upper Pokemouche, New Brunswick, the statue on top of the memorial stone is of the Virgin, while in St. Joachim, Ontario, near Windsor, it is once again an image of Christ. Possibly the most interesting example of the co-location of a religious statue and a soldiers' memorial is found in St. Pierre Jolys, Manitoba. In this town south of Winnipeg, the ultimate in nationalist soldier-saint martyrs, Joan of Arc, shares the monument with the figure of a pensive Canadian boy. She is in armour and holds a lance and banner, while he is dressed in a trench coat and leans on his rifle.

The integration of cenotaph and religious sculpture is not strictly a feature of Catholic communities. In Listowel, Ontario, a soldier kneels before an angel in the white marble statue on the monument. To the south of that town, in Norwich, Ontario, the memorial statue is an angel as well.

Iconoclasm is one of the major tenants in many Protestant churches. Calvinist austerity was a reaction against sanctuaries that were seen as overfilled with paintings, statues, and other religious objects. There was a strong tradition in Canada that favoured simplicity in religious matters. In a study of tombstone art in Puritan New England, a culture not unrelated to Protestant Canada, an American writer pointed out that religious art flourishes only when there is a great need for it.[8] The hardships, horrors, and staggering losses of the Great War left Canada in need of spiritual reassurance. That kind of social experience calls for a firm reaffirmation of faith and creating religious sculpture was part of the response, even in a culture that did not have a strong tradition of doing so. Because crucifixion scenes and statues of Christ himself would have been too much of a departure from Protestant ideas for most, there are many places, such as Greenspond, Newfoundland, Fenelon Falls, Ontario, Moose Jaw, Saskatchewan, and Duncan, British Columbia, where memorials took the form of plain crosses.

A measure of how affirmative Canadians were when they expressed their religious faith through monuments can be seen when we consider one of the

Plain crosses, such as this one on the island community of Greenspond, Newfoundland are found throughout Canada as war memorials. Shipley.

most universal characteristics of the country's memorials. Two traditions have been present in Christian funerary art through the ages. Historians have identified these as the representing of the departed person as though he was alive and the depiction of the deceased in a state of death.[9] The first style is motivated by a belief in the Resurrection and a faith that the person who has ended his physical existence on earth is in fact alive in Heaven. This form of funerary art is seen in the paintings and sculptures on the tombs of the early Christians, at a time when believers were still full of hope. The representation of people in death is more characteristic of periods of anxiety and precarious faith. In the Middle Ages, when the Black Death left Europe wondering whether humanity would survive at all, French nobles and Flemish businessmen had their tombs decorated with images of their corrupted and even decomposing bodies. Following the First World War there were many memorials in Europe that showed dead soldiers. There are *pieta* figures in France where a mother holds the body of her dead soldier-son. In London, England, the Artillery monument is an example of the representation of a fallen soldier in the tradition of the *"momento mori"* tomb. It is not hard to understand a certain depression among Europeans after a war in which they had almost committed communal suicide. But in Canada the mood, while remorseful, was marked by something quite different, and that difference is shown in the country's monuments. Almost all of the memorials in Canada conform to the more optimistic tradition in Christian tomb art, portraying soldiers as being alive. If the soldier figures are not actually alive on earth, they are being borne to Heaven, as the CPR memorials and the statue in Jacques Cartier, Quebec, indicate. Tellingly, one exception to this rule is found in St. Boniface, Manitoba, and it is not strictly speaking a Canadian memorial at all. It was commissioned by the Belgian community in that city; it commemorates men who fought and died in the Belgian service and so conforms more to the European mode.

Canadians who did not live through the First Great War and the time of monument building after it have sometimes mistaken the memorials for glorifications of war and martial values. There were no doubt some people who thought of victory when they saw the statue of a triumphant soldier on the main street of their town. But the evidence in the written record, the memorial inscriptions, and the visual symbolism of the monuments point to a much more religious motivation. Memorials were part of the attempt to make some sense on an emotional and spiritual level of the loss of so many friends, loved ones, and comrades. The unabsolved departed held an awesome power over the living, and the dead had to be answered. "If ye break faith with us who die," John McCrae's Flanders Field poem ends, "we shall not sleep." Not even the most charitable Canadian would contend that the sixty six thousand and fifty five shy farm boys, college students, and factory hands who died in the war were saints or Christlike to a man. They drank and swore and had all the vices of soldiers. They drowned in mud, wasted away with fever, and choked on poison gas. There was nothing glorious about their miserable deaths and it is unlikely that many had idealistic thoughts at the moments their limbs were torn off. But what people at home believed was that Canadian soldiers had done their best to serve the community in what they believed was its hour of need. Few understood the grand scale of events and fewer still had any ability to affect their course. They had not started the war and they could do nothing about its futile continuation. All they could do was serve and sacrifice. Christian symbolism was the traditional vocabulary that people called on to help them understand and express the value of selflessness that the soldiers embodied.

Christians believe that Christ sacrificed himself to redeem humanity. By his death he achieved immortality, but his suffering makes certain demands on us. We must live by his teachings. If the suffering and death of the soldiers was seen as their price for everlasting life, it also made demands on the survivors. To learn from and enshrine their example of service to society is the only way for us to vindicate their deaths. The monument in Summerside, Prince Edward Island, has an inscription that reads:

> O Canada the blood of all thy sons
> cries out today from fair and glorious deeds
> and spirit legions of immortal ones
> who died to serve their country and its needs
> pledge thee anew by their white honour roll
> to loftier issues born of sacrifice
> bidding thee keep unstained that nobler soul
> which they have ransomed with so great a price.[10]

On the base of a memorial cross in Cobourg, Ontario, a similar invocation is made:

> Standing beneath this Cross of Sacrifice
> we remember and must charge our children
> to remember that as our dead were equal in
> sacrifice so are they equal in honour for
> the greatest and the least of them have proved
> that sacrifice and honour are no vain things
> but truths by which the world lives.

The immense gift of life is recognized in the inscriptions on many other monuments as well. "There is no wealth but life," reads the memorial stone in Dauphin, Manitoba. Those killed "gave up the years to be, of work and joy and that unhoped serene, that men call age," says the inscription in Gaspé, Quebec.

A LA MEMOIRE
1914-18
CYRILE MAZEROLE
ANTOINE NOWLAN
CHARLES J ROBICHAUD
1939-45
CYRILE CAISSIE
RICHARD W BURBRIDGE
LUDGER LANDRY
ARTHUR DUGUAY

Religious statue and war memorial are one and the same in Upper Pochmouch, New Brunswick. Shipley.

St. Joan, one of the ultimate soldier saints, shares the memorial in St. Pierre, Manitoba with a pensive Canadian soldier. The plaque that has been added to the base commemorates not a soldier but a Mountie who was killed while on duty. Shipley.

The plaque in Ponoka, Alberta, tells us that "they died that we might live." Penticton, British Columbia, has one of the many cenotaphs that reminds us that "no greater love hath any man than he lay down his life for his friends." The specific values that people identified as having been preserved or defended were often carved in stone as well: "humanity, endurance, duty, sacrifice" are the four words inscribed on the four sides of the memorial at Oxdrift in northern Ontario. *"Morts pour la défense de la liberté et de la civilization,"* says the inscription in Lac-Megantic, Quebec. "For truth, justice, liberty," reads the stone in Mahone Bay, Nova Scotia.

In defence of these values, which are universal, the soldiers did not defeat an enemy so much as they defeated war itself. In Stratford, Ontario, the memorial inscription tells us, "They broke the sword and brought peace to our land." The cenotaph in Montreal salutes "the memory of the immortal dead who brought us honour and peace."

This rationale was never intended as an empty exercise in theology. Neither was it a ploy to absolve authorities of responsibility for the political failures that led to war. Monuments are not invocations of heavenly justification for bringing hell to earth. Canadian memorials, for all their religious dimension, do not say God was on our side. Our monuments were locally conceived and popularly supported; they were very real attempts to make everyday sense of exceptional tragedy, to turn abject futility into positive motivation, and to make future good of past wrong.

NINE
Nothing on Which
to Found a Country

The Canadians are marching
in impeccable formation,
every man in step.

The Canadians are marching.
Alden Nowlan: "Ypres: 1915"

Canada's battlefield leader in the First World War, Lieutenant-General Sir Arthur Currie, spoke to the crowd at the unveiling of the memorial cross in his home town, Strathroy, Ontario, in the summer of 1924. "War is not a means to establish peace. It is a delusion and a lie. To truly remember, we must take up the challenge to contend and sacrifice for the upbuilding of humanity. Canadians didn't fight for material gain but for an ideal. Ideals always have to be fought for and are never entirely won, that's the real message."[1] Monuments, Currie was saying, have to do with people's thoughts and feelings, and those are constantly changing. The way memorials are treated depends on whether they continue to reflect current thinking and whether their statement continues to be heard and understood by the community.

Throughout the First World War, and most especially during the last desperate movements, large numbers of German weapons were captured by Canadian troops. In accordance with ancient custom these guns were dragged home by the victorious to be displayed as trophies of war. The Dominion archivist, Sir Arthur Doughty, was busy collecting documents relating to the war and it was he who was put in charge of distributing the booty. As befitted his profession, Doughty kept a careful register of where each gun had been captured, by what unit, and where in Canada it was sent.[2] We find, for example, that the 44th

(opposite) Signs of serious deterioration are visible in the marble of the statue in Priceville, Ontario. The blade of the weapon on the belt may have been broken off by vandals or it may have been originally carved that way. In ancient times harolds of peace carried broken swords. Street.

Battalion of the Canadian Expeditionary Force took a trench mortar and a machine-gun on September 27, 1918, during the crossing of the Canal du Nord. On October 20, 1920, after crossing the ocean, these items were sent by train to the village of Bayfield, Ontario.

The demand for war trophies was astonishing. Hundreds of letters from cities, towns, Indian bands, schools, Red Cross societies, and every other kind of group flowed across Doughty's desk. Students at the Ontario Agricultural College at Guelph signed a petition requesting a gun. T. Sims, reeve of the southwestern Ontario village of West Lorne, wrote asking the government to send a war trophy "provided it was not one of those little fellows."[3] The Agricultural College received a 105 mm. field gun in April 1921, and West Lorne got a trench mortar and two machine-guns in September 1920. By the time the distribution was complete, three thousand four hundred and fifty German guns were sitting in front of court houses, town halls, and memorial hospitals across Canada. At Farnham and Granby, Quebec, captured artillery pieces were placed on pedestals and used as monuments. The machine-gun that was sent to Weymouth, Nova Scotia, was placed on top of the memorial stone, as was the one that went to Douglas, Manitoba. Each of these guns was accompanied by a letter from the Director of War Trophies. "These trophies, which have been declared the property of the people of Canada, are sent to you with the understanding that proper care will be taken of them and in taking them over, it is understood that you agree to this condition."[4]

In spite of the enthusiasm for war trophies that was evident in the flush of victory and the official direction to take care of them, the vast majority have since disappeared. The two in Farnham and Granby, Quebec, were replaced by stones that stand on the pedestals originally occupied by the guns. A letter from the Vancouver Parks Commission to the local military commander indicates that even by 1933 there were problems with the war trophies:

> In view of the fact that the condition of certain of the Guns on exhibit in various parks in the City is such as to render them a source of public danger, especially to children who persist in playing with them and climb over them, and the Board having been advised in one particular instance of at least two children who have suffered injuries, the Board decided at its last regular meeting that something would have to be done to remedy such hazards and instructed me to take steps to have these guns removed.[5]

A few years later, when shortages of metal during the Second World War prompted salvage drives all over the country, any source of scrap was welcomed. Metal fences came down, old streetcar tracks were torn up, and many of the war trophies were melted down. The guns in Bayfield, Guelph, and West Lorne,

In Frank, Alberta, as in many places in the country, the captured German guns that served as memorials or parts of memorials after World War I are now removed or in poor repair. Shipley.

Ontario, were among some six hundred and seventy-six, or twenty per cent, of the original trophies that were officially known to have been designated as salvage. Most of the rest have simply been allowed to rust away over the years. The wooden wheels of the field pieces rot, and more and more of them slowly disappear. The ones in Weymouth, Nova Scotia, and Douglas, Manitoba, are among the few left.[6]

The need for scrap and the hazards posed for playing children may explain the immediate reasons why objects once so sought after were later removed. A more fundamental issue was that guns and other military hardware were inappropriate as memorials. At first the presence of captured enemy arms was a visible indication of victory, but the elation was transitory. After a while the cold, hard steel simply brought back visions of the very struggle and slaughter that both the bereaved population and the returned veterans wanted to forget. It was the idea of service and sacrifice that people wanted to remember and honour, not victory and the acts of war itself.[7]

What was appropriate, judging from the types of memorials that have lasted longest, was something that employed ancient and well-known symbols to convey the more profound lessons that war had engraved on the public conscience. It is the solemn, serious, even religious message contained in memorials that allows them to transcend a particular time and remain meaningful.

More recent monuments, such as this one in Beiseker, Alberta sometimes feature weapons of war. That was almost never the case with those that have survived from the period following World War I. Shipley.

Even that, however, has not been enough to ensure the continued existence of and respect for monuments. Just as the war trophies initially used as memorials were officially removed or neglected and allowed to decay, so a certain number of the more permanent monuments have suffered abuse both intentional and unavoidable.

In the Canadian climate the elements ravage any exposed objects. The heat of summer in British Columbia valleys, the prairie winds, the winter frosts in Quebec, and the salt spray in the Atlantic coastal towns all work their mischief. Marble was chosen for statues and memorial stones because of its initial beauty and its exotic appeal, but never for its durability. Over a hundred turns of the seasons have left Italian marble figures on Toronto's Fenian Raids Memorial almost featureless. A similar fate awaits the dozens of other marble soldiers across the country. The memorial figure in Canmore, Alberta, was erected in the 1920s. By the 1970s it was in such poor shape that it was removed from the main street and relegated to the town's cemetery. In Assiniboia, Saskatchewan, the decaying marble statue was taken off the monument and thrown away. Other marble sculptures are chipped and stained with dark streaks. In places such as Charlottetown, Newfoundland, where there is no statue but where they do have marble memorial stones, the inscriptions are slowly being worn smooth. In communities with cairns of fieldstone or cenotaphs constructed of granite blocks the pointing or mortar that holds them together can deteriorate until the

This monument in St. Boniface, Manitoba is almost unique in Canada in portraying a dead soldier. It was erected by the Belgian community in honour of those of their countrymen who returned home to fight in World War I. The crumbling state of the sculpture gives it a particularly macabre appearance. Shipley.

memorials crumble. In 1978 a cairn in Charlton, Ontario, had reached this point, while the plaque on a similar monument in Gibbons, Alberta, had fallen off.

Vandalism presents another major threat to monuments in Canadian communities. Precisely because of their central location and the fact that they are often surrounded by parks, memorial sites became the gathering places of the bored and the under-employed. There is a sense that monuments represent values central to the society from which they feel alienated. To those who sit around them the memorials have sometimes become targets for their frustration.

Memorials have not been free either from official moves to destroy or alter them. An arch built in the 1930s in Niagara Falls, Ontario, commemorating the victims of the 1837 Rebellion, was torn down in the 1960s to improve traffic flow. The decorative panels were stored away and plans to rebuild the arch elsewhere were never carried out. While the complete destruction of monuments has not yet become common, some have been moved out of the centres of towns and modified in controversial ways.

The various ongoing threats to the existence of memorials means that they survive only because enough people continue to think them important. Sometimes a single individual is primarily responsible for the care of a memorial. James Watson sculpted the statue in Trenton, Nova Scotia, from a large piece of fairly soft sandstone taken from a quarry in nearby Wallace. Every couple of years he has put a coat of liquid silicon on the figure to help preserve it against the weather. Watson can not help wondering who will do it after him.

In many places the Canadian Legion looks after the routine maintenance of the local monument. There are cases as well where a Legion Branch will take care of a monument in some community nearby when no other group is doing it. The work of the Legion in this regard is admirable and clearly seen by it as its duty, but it has the unfortunate side-effect of reinforcing the notion in the minds of some that memorials are of interest only to veterans.

Municipal authorities, through their parks departments, undertake the upkeep of numerous other memorials, particularly in larger centres. A resolution from a meeting of the city council in St. Catharines, Ontario, in October 1982, shows that one thousand four hundred and twenty dollars was allocated for the general cleaning and repair of two missing lead letters on one of the monuments in that city.[8] Even when public bodies are charged with the care of monuments, however, there are still questions of who should bear the costs. The Toronto Historical Board had to apply to the Province of Ontario in the 1970s, for example, for funds to stabilize the deteriorating marble on the Fenian Raids Memorial in the city.[9]

*Vandalism is a problem for monuments not just in Griswald, Manitoba, but all over Canada.
Shipley.*

A further problem for those interested in protecting monuments lies in the present state of the technology. There are several possible approaches to the preservation of exposed stone and bronze objects, but no one is foolproof, sure, or clearly favoured. Some methods that have actually been used can even be harmful in the long run. Where stone has been painted, moisture becomes trapped under the paint and causes further damage when it freezes and thaws.

Along with considerations of caring for the actual material from which monuments are made, there is also the question of caring for the symbolic aspects. Memorials were generally erected in the centres of communities to underline their central significance. Rapid changes in the urban landscape of many places, especially in the expanding West, meant that some monuments were no longer at the focal points of the communities. In Edmonton, Alberta, and Saskatoon, Saskatchewan, people noted this change. In both places the cenotaphs have been moved in recent years, not out of places of importance but back into them reflecting the original intent.

Another way that the symbolic importance of memorials has been recognized in urban planning can be seen where towns have been relocated for some reason. The sites of several eastern Ontario communities were flooded in the 1950s as a result of the construction of the St. Lawrence Seaway. Towns such as

Woodrow, Saskatchewan is probably home to fewer people now than it was during the World Wars. But the monument to the community's lost remains. Shipley.

Morrisburg, Ontario, were partially or wholly relocated, while other places such as Inglewood, Ontario, were entirely new creations where people from several small flooded hamlets were relocated. In all cases, however, the war memorials were moved from old locations into symbolically significant and central spots in the new settlements. A monument was also moved from Natal, British Columbia, to the new townsite of Sparwood when Natal and Michel were abandoned in the southeastern B.C. coal mining district. In this case the two pillars of the monument were probably mixed up during reconstruction since the alphabetical list of names begins on the right-hand pillar instead of the left-hand one.

A further indication of what the future might possibly hold in store for monuments is seen in the way they have become intertwined with our whole perception of the past. Most monuments originated as commemorations of a particular event or series of events. For most, but not all, communities the immediate event commemorated was the First World War. Some places did not get around to building war memorials until later, but when they did so they were filling a gap or correcting an oversight.[10] In these cases the dates and perhaps names from both world wars were included. The monument, in other words, remembered the ideals and the sacrifices of people whenever they had served. The monuments became general tributes to all who have gone before. In Delaware, near London, Ontario, a recently built memorial carries the designation and dates of all the conflicts in which Canada has been involved, from the War of 1812 to Korea. The area around Delaware was raided by the Americans in 1813 and probably represents one of the deepest penetrations that an invader ever made into Canada. The inscription says: "The freedoms, advantages and standards of the present were paid for by the industry, hardship and sacrifices of the people of the past." In McLean, Saskatchewan, and Poplar Hill, Ontario, the memorials reach out to include a recognition of the people who settled the country as well. In Redwater, Alberta, the memorial inscription reads:

> In memoriam to those who have given
> their lives in defence of their country;
> In memoriam of the pioneers of this district.
> If ye break faith with us who die
> We shall not sleep.

In St. Pierre, Manitoba, the memorial originally dedicated to the soldiers who died in the First World War also reaches forward to include the service of a local Mountie killed while on duty in 1971.

This recognition of the debt to the past that is embodied so well in many memorials in Canada is also captured in the lines of Alden Nowlan's poem, "Ypres: 1915."[11] The fact that the First World War still has the power to inspire

Canadian poets and the fact that the memorials still command awe even without people understanding why is a measure of the impact that the war had on our society. Nowlan's poem speaks of the Canadians who faced history's first gas attack. The cloud of poisonous vapour came towards them like a metaphor for all the worst things that modern technology had waiting for twentieth century man. But with a "stubborn disinclination" Nowlan's Private MacNally, who could have been the unknown soldier on any of the hundreds of statues in the country, refused to give up his trench even in the face of death. The poem concludes:

> And that's ridiculous, too, and nothing
> on which to found a country
>   still
> It makes me feel good, knowing
> that in some obscure, conclusive way
> they were connected with me
> and me with them.

All that remains of ghost town, Phoenix, British Columbia, is its war memorial. PABC.

Societies, civilizations, and nations come and go. All that is left now of the cultures that were Ancient Egypt, Imperial China, and Rome are their monuments. In our country there are a few places where time has been foreshortened. Worked-out mines, abandoned rail lines, and changing land use have left once thriving communities empty. It might be the eventual fate of all our cities, the way it was of so many in the past. In Phoenix, British Columbia, Bankhead, Alberta, and New Jerusalem, New Brunswick, the people and even most of the buildings are gone. Virtually all that is left in these places are the war memorials. Each has a list of names of the people who died in service. If those people are remembered, as Sir Arthur Currie implored, by our taking up "the challenge to contend and sacrifice for the upbuilding of humanity," and if we keep the memorials to remind us that "ideals always have to be fought for and are never entirely won," then something has been accomplished by Canadians in correcting the wrongs of war. And if all that remains one day of our society are the monuments that now stand in the centres of our towns and represent those ideals of service, then we could have done worse.

The central and special position given to war monuments in Canadian communities can be seen in this view of North Vancouver, British Columbia. Street.

APPENDIX A
Glossary

In this book certain general principles and ideas concerning war memorials in Canada are outlined and discussed. Examples are drawn from all over the country to illustrate points but only a small fraction of the monuments that exists are actually described. To help those who want to better understand the memorials in their own communities the following list of terms and descriptions is offered.

Allegorical Figures: Sometimes sculptures of humans or human-like figures are used in memorial art to represent ideas or concepts. The winged angels that appear on many of our memorials, for example, are allegories or representations of the heavenly spirit. Other figures represent war or barbarism or heroism. (p. 67)

Altar: A flat-topped block on which sacrificial offerings are made to a deity. In the Christian church the altar is the communion table where the Eucharist is celebrated. In memorial art there is often a representative altar which symbolizes the sacrificial offering of the soldiers' lives. (p. 140)

Attributes: In the symbolism of Christian art the saints are usually pictured holding some article that identifies them. St. Peter carries the keys since he is the keeper of the gates of heaven and St. Luke holds a pen because he is the patron saint of doctors and artists. When soldiers are portrayed in saint-like postures on our monuments they also hold identifying attributes such as their rifles and the crosses that mark their graves. (p. 145)

Auf Vif: The tradition in tomb art of presenting the dead as they were in life (see *Transi*). This style is considered as representing a society that is fairly optimistic about its chances of salvation.

Balmoral: A soft, flat cap worn by some Scottish regiments. (pp. 60, 132)

Bandoleer: This is a belt for carrying ammunition and is worn over the shoulder. Since it was seldom a part of Canadian gear during the First World War, its appearance on a statue can indicate the sculpture's foreign origin. On statues from the Boer War it is an accurate representation of the equipment our soldiers might have used. (p. 42)

Barret: A small, flat cap that became common issue among Canadian troops in the Second World War.

Bayonet: This is the long knife that is attached to the end of a rifle or musket to make it into a spear-like weapon. Because they are the thinest projecting part of many statues of soldiers holding guns they are often found bent or broken off by vandals. (p. 78)

Bearskin: Various styles of tall fur hats have been worn as part of military uniforms. The bearskin is associated particularly with Guards regiments while other types such as astrakhans and buzbies were traditionally worn by other kinds of troops. At the end of the nineteenth century they disappeared for all but ceremonial purposes but there are monuments in Canada with statues wearing fur hats.

Broken Chain: The chain can be a symbol of death and the broken chain emblematic of life's triumph over death. A chain can also be seen as symbolizing slavery and, when broken, a symbol of victory over tyranny.

Broken Sword: Traditionally the heralds who served as go-betweens during negotiations between warring armies carried broken swords. That indicated that they were non-combatants or messengers of peace. In our memorials broken swords, either carried by sculptural figures or lying at the base of monuments, indicate the idea of peace. (p. 160)

Cairn: One of the oldest and most common ways for humans to mark a place, for any reason, is to pile up stones. Many of the monuments in Canada consist of such stone piles, often cemented together with a plaque affixed to them. (p. 102)

Calvary: This was the traditional place of execution outside Biblical Jerusalem and came from the Latin word for skull either because of the shape of the hill or because it was associated with death. The name in Greek was Golgotha, which was derived from the original Aramaic. Accord-

(opposite) Monuments such as Montreal's cenotaph are alive as symbols. Using them as the focus for ongoing concerns is not without controversy, however. Street.

ing to the Bible there were three crosses on the hill when Christ was executed and often three crosses appear in sculpture and represent Calvary. In Christian countries, especially France, small shrines featuring a crucifix were also called Calvaries. Particularly in rural areas war memorials sometimes have the appearance of Calvaries in the sense of a shrine.

Campaign Hat: The broad-brimmed hat that we usually associate with the Mounted Police or boy scouts was worn by many Canadian soldiers, particularly cavalrymen, during the Boer War. (p. 42)

Carrara Marble: Much of the beautiful but soft and easily weathered marble that was used in monuments in Canada came from the famous ancient marble quarries near Florence in northern Italy. (p. 160)

Celtic Cross: A style of cross that generally had relatively short top and side projections and often a circle connecting its four arms was associated with ancient Scotland and Ireland and named after the Celts who were the early inhabitants of those places. Another feature of Celtic art was the intertwined linear design and the crosses are often decorated with such patterns both in the old country and in their Canadian descendants. (pp. 12, 117)

Cenotaph: The word comes from the Greek roots meaning "empty" and "tomb." Although cenotaph is often used in Canada to indicate a simple stone pylon as opposed to a monument with sculpture, any memorial could be called a cenotaph in that it is a tomb where the bodies of those remembered are not actually placed and in the sense that Christ's tomb was empty after the resurrection.

Classical Architecture: Much of the decoration on monuments is derived from the architecture of ancient Greece and Rome. Since the Renaissance in fifteenth and sixteenth century Italy these forms had been used by builders. There are three main orders or styles of classical architecture (Doric, Ionic, and Corinthian) each with its own particular variations on the same basic theme. When these architectural details appear on monuments in Canada they are seldom in a pure state but it helps to know the models they are derived from so that we can describe them.

1. *Column* - The principal feature of classical architecture is the column. It probably derived from the use of tree trunks to support roofs but after a certain point they were made of stone. (p. 22)

   Pilaster - This is a column that is not free-standing but projects in relief from the side of a structure and is purely decorative rather than structural.

2. *Capital* - This is the top portion of a column and the most obvious difference between the orders of architecture. Doric capitals are very plain, Ionic ones have a scroll design while Corinthian capitals are highly decorated.

3. *Base* - The drum on which the columns rest are also distinctive in each order.

4. *Entablature* - This is the upper part of an architectural order and has several constituent parts.

5. *Cornice* - The crowning, projecting part of the entablature.

6. *Architrave* - The main horizontal beam that rests on top of the columns.

7. *Frieze* - In a horizontal line above the architrave there is often a decorative band. In the Ionic and Corinthian orders this is often a continuous band of relief sculpture, although frieze can also refer to any elongated band of sculptural relief. In the Doric order the frieze has at least two distinct parts.

8. *Trigliph* - A pattern of three vertical lines that is repeated over and over on the frieze in the Doric order.

9. *Metope* - The space between the trigliphs in which there were sometimes sculpted scenes.

10. *Dentils* - A series of small tooth-like projections found under the cornice in the Ionic and Corinthian orders.

Collar Dogs: The badges worn on the collars of Canadian uniforms. They were usually metal during the First World War. Some indicated the Canadian Expeditionary Force Battalion number and company designation while others were simply small versions of the cap badge. Most often they show up as maple leaves on the statues of soldiers since the majority of badges were based on that symbol. In Newfoundland the collar dogs and badges show their insignia, the caribou. (p. 110)

Crown and Cross: In Christian iconography the cross inside a crown is used to signify the notion of trading the cross of earthly suffering for the crown of eternal life.

Cross of Sacrifice: Following the First World War the Imperial (later the Commonwealth) War Graves Commission was established. They were charged with the care of the cemeteries both on the battlefields and wherever veterans were buried. Sir Reginald Blomfield was one of the British architects who was asked to design special memorials. His Cross of Sacrifice with its practical short arms and the bronze sword attached became the standard central marker in cemeteries and was widely imitated. (p. 64)

Crusader Sword: The medieval sword shaped like a cross and symbolized the battle, both spiritual and physical, of good against evil. (p. 100)

Dove: This bird has a strong Judeo-Christian tradition as a symbol of both peace and the connection between God and man. In the Bible when the great flood was subsiding Noah sent out a dove. The bird returned with an olive branch signaling that the devastation of the world was over. In the New Testament the spirit of God descends on Christ in the form of a dove when he is baptized by John.

Drapery: Various representations of fabric drapery often form part of the decoration on monuments. In the simplest reading this is just a carry-over from the days in antiquity when austere buildings were festooned with bunting for special occasions. However, in the symbolic context drapery might signify Christ's garment or even his shroud. The soldiers who crucified Christ drew lots for his garment, which could be seen as referring to the worthlessness of earthly possessions, while the shroud was left behind by the risen Christ.

Eternal Flame: The idea of keeping a flame burning forever in remembrance of fallen soldiers became popular after the First World War, but as with so many symbolic gestures, the notion has deep cultural roots. When Greeks colonized new areas in the ancient world they took with them sacred fires from the temples in their home cities. The Jewish celebration of Hanukkah recalls an incident in the time of the Maccabean Revolt (2nd Cent. B.C.) when the temple lamps were miraculously kept burning. In a few places in Canada there are actual burning flames but more often there is a stone or bronze representation. (p. 117)

Flanders Cross: Before the introduction of the stone grave markers that are now found in the Commonwealth War Graves Commission cemeteries in Europe, the resting places of soldiers were marked with temporary wooden crosses. One of the designs, which had reinforcements between the arms of the cross, is sometimes used in sculptures on memorials. (p. 145)

Forage Cap: The design probably originated in the peasant hats of central and eastern Europe and was worn by some German troops during the Napoleonic Wars. At the time of the First World War this brimmed cap was in general use in the Canadian and other British inspired armies. It was worn in combat at the beginning of the war before being replaced by the steel helmet. Unlike more recent versions, the First World War forage cap was quite soft and with continuous wear tended to become rather idiosyncratic in shape. This meant that in some sculptural representations the forage caps on the soldiers look very odd. Many of these sculptures were done in Italy from photographs which is another explanation of the strange shaped caps. (p. 2)

Furled Flag: Battle flags, or colours, as they are called in the army, are symbols of unity and fighting spirit. In previous times their presence on the battlefield provided a rallying point. When they are furled or gathered it is in respectful salute or when they are retired to a sanctuary. As decorations on monuments they convey this sense of withdrawal from combat. (pp. 84, 105)

Garrison Cap (Wedge Cap): A small, rather impractical military hat that covers little of the head. They appeared in the nineteenth century and remain part of the Canadian military uniform. Some Boer War period statues wear them but they are probably most strongly associated with the RCAF in the Second World War.

Glengarry: The Scottish version of the wedge cap which usually has two long ribbons hanging down at the back.

Hackle: A feather decoration worn on military hats. The name comes from the feathers on the neck of a bird of prey which stand up when they fight. (p. 132)

Insignia: Representations of various badges and coats of arms appear on Canadian monuments. Some are regimental or battalion insignia on the uniforms and caps of soldier sculptures. Others are detailed reproductions of badges on the bases of statues or other monuments. As well some communities have the municipal coat of arms as part of the memorial. (p. 117)

Keystone: The central block at the apex of a stone arch is the one that all the others rest on. Both because of its structural and symbolic position it is sometimes decorated and made a central point of the design. (p. 139)

Latin Cross: This is the most standard cross design in which the bottom part of the vertical bar is longer than the other three arms. (p. 154)

Laurel: In ancient times, branches of the laurel bush were woven into crowns or wreaths that were presented to victorious athletes and generals as symbols of triumph. It Christian iconography this victory sign came to mean the triumph of life over death. (p. 108)

Maltese Cross: This is a cross with four short and equal arms.

Maple Leaf: By the middle of the nineteenth century the maple leaf had started to emerge as a distinctively Canadian emblem. During the First World War a great many of the battalions raised for overseas service used variations of the maple leaf as their badges and afterwards it appeared on many war memorials (see Strom Galloway, *Canadian Geographic*, 102, June/July, 1982, pp. 30-35).

Menhirs: Tall, rough-hewn upright stones found in northern France and the British Isles. These prehistoric monuments are thought to have figured in the religious life of the ancients and in numerous cases they came to have a special significance for the early Christians. Many memorials in Canada were made to look like these ancient standing stones. (p. 105)

Mortar: An artillery piece, often of quite small calibre, that fires on a very high trajectory, lobbing its explosive charge at the target. Mortars of different types were used as decorative motifs on some monuments, perhaps because they were small and compact but conveyed the idea of military hardware.

Obelisk: A tall, tapering stone shaft that had its stylistic origin in ancient Egypt but which has been widely used as a monument in the modern world. (pp. 81, 101)

Olive Branch: A traditional symbol of peace and reconciliation (see *Dove*).

Our Lady: Statues of the Virgin Mary have been used as part of war memorials in some places in Canada. The Virgin is traditionally associated with peace and reconciliation. She is often pictured treading on a snake, since she is the second Eve who will finally overcome the original sin that was initiated by the serpent's temptation. It may be, however, that the use of statues of Our Lady for war memorials had more to do with the availability of such sculptures than with any particular symbolism relating to war and peace. (p. 157)

Palm Fronds: Like the laurel, the palm frond was an ancient symbol of triumph that indicated victory of life over death in Christian symbolism. They are particularly associated with Christ's triumphal entry into Jerusalem on Palm Sunday. (p. 106)

Pickelhaube: The spiked helmet worn by German troops from the eighteenth century on was imitated by British forces in the style we usually associate with English policemen. Such helmets were worn in Canada around the time of the Riel Rebellion and there are statues of our soldiers wearing them. While not made of metal, they were heavier than the pith helmet associated with the Boer War.

Pith Helmet: A light, tropical sun hat made from dried sola and covered with canvas that was worn by the infantry and artillery in the Boer War.

Plinth: The base of a statue.

Poppy: Although the poppy owed much of its popularity as a remembrance symbol after the First World War to John McCrae's poem *In Flanders Fields*, it had long been associated with Christ's passion and with rebirth. (p. 145)

Putties: The woolen wrapping worn by soldiers around their legs. (p. 145)

Relief: A sculpture that is not freestanding but raised to some extent from a flat background. We sometimes refer to a relief sculpture as a plaque. (pp. 20-21)

Resting on Arms Reversed: The military drill position in which a soldier, with his head bowed, rests his hands on the butt of his rifle while the muzzle is resting on the ground. It is the position of mourning and during a military funeral four soldiers stand at the corners of the coffin resting on arms reversed. A similar configuration is usually adopted around a cenotaph on Remembrance Day. (p. 118)

St. Andrew's Cross: According to tradition, St. Andrew was martyred on a cross that he asked to be turned on its side so that he would not presume to be crucified like Christ. Since St. Andrew is the patron saint of Scotland, this X-shaped cross is identified with that country. Canadian Scottish regiments usually have a St. Andrew's Cross in their insignia.

Sam Brown: The nickname of the brown leather belt that was worn around the waist and over the shoulder by army officers. In some places in Canada the figures in memorial sculptures wear them. (p. 60)

Sarcophagus: A decorated coffin. In ancient times bodies were actually buried in ornate sarcophagi but eventually they become simply symbolic. They sometimes appear on Canadian war memorials as symbols of the dead given an honoured and respected burial.

Shrine: A few war memorials are built in the form of small chapels (see *Calvary*). (p. 109)

Star of David: The six-pointed star that is the symbol of Judaism is used in the same way as the Christian cross on monuments that commemorate Jewish servicemen.

Stele (pl. Stelia): An upright slab of stone used as a monument or grave marker. This simple type of memorial probably originated in ancient Greece. (p. 107)

Swags: Strings of flowers used as decorations. Originally these may have had some symbolic connection to rites of spring or may have been connected with the worship of fertility deities or other gods but they have survived only with a general ornamental significance. (p. 172)

Torch: The idea of a torch symbolizing the light carried in the search for truth was an ancient one, but like the poppy it was popularized during the First World War by McCrae's poem *In Flanders Fields*. He said, "To you from falling hands we throw/ The torch; be yours to hold it high." (see *Eternal Flame*). (p. 73)

Transi: The style of tomb art that portrayed the dead either as they appeared in death or even in advanced states of decomposition. It originated in the late Middle Ages in Flanders and France and was symptomatic of a depressed and morbid outlook in society (see *Auf Vif*). (pp. 148, 165)

Trenches: Intricate networks of ditches were the major feature of the front lines during the First World War. These trenches were reinforced with sandbags and the bottoms were often covered with wooden platforms called duck-boards to allow the men to walk over the ubiquitous mud. In the statues on war memorials sandbags and duck-boards sometime appear to give a hint of the environment in which the soldiers fought. (p. 73)

Unit Patches: As well as cap badges and collar dogs, Canadian soldiers in the First World War were identified by a system of cloth patterns that were sewn to their tunic sleeves. There were coloured squares indicating the division and triangles, half circles, and so on to designate the brigade and battalion. These patches are visible on some memorial statues. (p. 110)

War Trophies: Throughout the First World War and especially near the end enemy weapons were captured by Canadian troops. Large numbers of these were transported home as war trophies according to an ancient right of victory. Hundreds were allocated to cities, towns, schools, hospitals, and clubs all over the country. Many were displayed as part of community war memorials. During the Second World War great numbers of them were melted down for scrap and subsequently many rusted away and were removed. Very few remain in their original locations. (p. 163)

Web Gear: The belts, packs, and pouches worn by Canadian soldiers in this century are known collectively as webbing from the coarse weave of the fabric from which they were made. The statues on memorials often wear various combinations of web gear from a simple belt and bayonet case all the way to the full marching order that included a backpack, water canteen, and entrenching tool. The latter was an item of questionable utility that consisted of a small shovel-like blade and a detachable wooden handle that was carried next to the bayonet. (pp. 110, 124, 135)

APPENDIX B
List of Monuments

The following is a list of cities, towns and villages by province and territory which have memorials about which the author collected at least some information during the time this book was being researched. It concludes with a list of overseas memorials built by the Commonwealth War Graves Commission, many of which have also been visited by the author. The list does not pretend to include *all* Canadian war monuments inside and outside the country but probably represents the majority. The author's files are now in the Public Archives of Canada, where they are available for research and the addition of further information.

Especially in larger centres there is often more than one monument. In these cases the different monuments are either described, the conflict or war commemorated named, the group honoured identified, the location of the the monument given or any of these variables combined. When there is more than one monument the main civic memorial is referred to as the "cenotaph." In all other cases a one or two word description of it is given unless the monument defies such a brief account or the form is unknown to the author.

It is stressed again that this is not a complete list of Canadian war memorials. Any additional information known by readers should be sent to the Publich Archives of Canada, 395 Wellington St., Ottawa.

ALBERTA
Banff - plaque
Bankhead - stele
Beiseker - stele
Bentley - arch
Big Valley - cairn
Blairmore - stele
Bowden - cairn
Burdett - cairn
Calgary
  Boer War - statue
  cenotaph - stone shaft
  Burnside Cemetery - cross
  Currie Barracks - metal cairn
  Ogden CPR shops - cairn
  137th Battalion - cairn
  Queen's Park Veterans' Cemetery-stele
Camrose - obelisk
Canmore - statue
Cardston - stele
Cochrane - cairn
Coleman - statue
Coronation - cairn
Cremona - cairn
Drumheller - cenotaph - stone shaft
Eaglesham - cairn

Edmonton
  cenotaph - stone shaft
  Cross of Sacrifice - cemetery
  Jasper Place Legion
Edson - cairn
Foremost - cairn
Fort MacLeod - stone structure
Frank - gun
Gadsby - small arch
Gibbons - cairn
Hinton - cross
Innisfall
  town centre - cairn
  cemetery-cairn
Jasper - cairn
Lacombe - statue
Leduc - cairn
Lethbridge
  cenotaph - statue
  Mountain View Cemetery - eternal flame
Mannville - stele
Medicine Hat - statue
Morinville - concrete pillars
Olds - cairn
Pincher Creek - statue
Ponoka - cairn
Redcliff - brick column

Red Deer
  cenotaph - statue
  RCAF - cairn
Redwater - pyramid
Rimbey - stele
St. Albert - sarcophagus
St. Paul - obelisk
Stettler - obelisk
Taber - statue
Three Hills - cross
Trochu - cairn
Two Hills - cairn
Vegreville - stele
Vermilion - cairn
Wainwright - tower
Wetaskiwin - stone pillars
Wildwood - cairn

BRITISH COLUMBIA
Abbotsford - cairn
Aldergrove - cairn
Armstrong - stone shaft
Bowen Island - cairn
Burnaby - obelisk
Campbell River - small stone
Castlegar - cross
Chemainus - obelisk
Chilliwack - stone shaft
Cloverdale
Colwood - cairn

Courtenay - cairn
Cranbrook - obelisk
Creston - stone shaft
Duncan - cenotaph cross
North Cowichan - tower
Enderby - obelisk
Esquimalt
    cenotaph - flagpole base
    cemetery - Cross of
        Sacrifice
Fernie
    cenotaph - statue
    cemetery - altar
Fort Langley - cross
Fruitvale - cairn
Ganges - obelisk
Golden - cairn
Grand Forks - obelisk
Greenwood - pyramid
Haney - cross
Hedley - obelisk
Holden - sculpture
Hope - large stone
Houston - cairn
Invermere - cairn
Kamloops
    clock tower
    IODE - pyramid
Kaslo - obelisk
Keremeos - cairn
Kimberley - cairn
Ladysmith - large stone
Lytton - cairn
Malakwa - cairn
Mayne Island - arch
Merritt - stone shaft
Mission - stele
Nanaimo - stone structure
Nelson - obelisk
New Westminster - statue
North Vancouver - stone shaft
Oliver - cairn
Osoyoos - cairn
Parksville - cross
Peachland - obelisk
Pemberton - cross
Penticton - obelisk
Phoenix - stele
Port Alberni - concrete
    structure
Port Moody - stucco shaft
Prince Rupert - stone shaft
Princeton - pyramid
Qualicum Beach - wooden
    maple leaf
Quamichan - cross

Revelstoke - stone shaft
Rossland - obelisk
Salmo - brick wall
Salmon Arm - cairn
Sidney - cairn
Sparwood - arch
Summerland - stone shaft
Trail - stone shaft
Vancouver
    cenotaph - stone shaft
    CPR station - statue
    Grandview Legion - cairn
    Japanese-Canadians -
        column
    South Hill - stone shaft
Vedder Crossing - stone shaft
Vernon - stone shaft
Victoria
    cenotaph - statue
    Cathedral - cross
    Oak Bay - statue
    Royal Roads Military
        College - stone shaft
West Vancouver - arch

MANITOBA
Alexander - stone shaft
Arborg - brick wall
Arden - statue
Baldur - cairn
Basswood - standing stone
Belmont - tower
Binscarth - statue
Birds Hill - obelisk
Birtle - stone shaft
Boissevain - statue
Bowsman - cairn
Brandon
    armoury - stone block
    cemetery - cross
    Old City Hall - cairn
Carberry - statue
Cartwright - obelisk
Churchill - cairn
Clanwilliam - obelisk
Clearwater - cairn
Crandall - cairn
Crystal City - obelisk
Darlingford - chapel
Deloraine - arch
Dominion City - stele
Douglas - cairn and gun
Edrans - stele
Elgin - standing stone
Elkhorn - obelisk

Elm Creek - obelisk
Emerson - statue
Erickson - cairn
Forest - stone pillar
Foxwarren - statue
Franklin - obelisk
Garson Quarry - obelisk
Gilbert Plains - stele
Gimli
    cenotaph - cairn
    Lakeside Camp - stone
        shaft
Gladstone - statue
Glenboro - obelisk
Grandview - cairn
Griswold - obelisk
Grunthal - statues
Hamiota - statue
Hartney - stone shaft
Holland - statue
Kelwood - statue
Killarney - statue
Langruth - obelisk
McCreary - stele
MacGregor - statue
Manitou - statue
Margaret - statue
Melita - flag pole
Miami - obelisk
Miniota - stone shaft
Minitonas - obelisk
Minnedosa - obelisk
Minto - cairn
Moline - cairn
Moosehorn - cairn
Morden - statue
Morris - obelisk
Newdale - statue
Ninette - obelisk
North Kildonan - stele
Oak Lake - cross
Oak River - cairn
Oakbank - statue
The Pas - stone shaft
Pilot Mound - obelisk
Pine Falls - cairn
Plumas - arch
Portage la Prairie - statue
Rapid City - cairn
Rathwell - obelisk
Reston - statue
Riding Mountain - cairn
Rivers - statue
Roblin - statue
Roland - statue

Rossburn - statue
St. Adolphe - stele
St. Andrews - arch
St. Boniface
   Coronation Park - stone
     shaft
   Belgian cenotaph - statue
   French cenotaph - statue
St. Claude - statues
St. James
   Bruce Park - stone shaft
   Legion - stele
St. Laurent - cairn
St. Norbert - cross
St. Pierre - statues
St. Vital - stele
Sandy Lake - stele
Sanford - cairn
Selkirk - stele
Shoal Lake - stele
Snowflake - cairn
Souris - cross
Sperling - cairn
Steinbach - stele
Stonewall - stone shaft
Stony Mountain - cairn
Strathclair - stele
Swan River
   Birchwood cemetery - stele
   cenotaph - cairn
Teulon - obelisk
Thompson - stele
Transcona - obelisk
Treesbank - kiosk
Treherne - statue
Tyndall - obelisk
Virden - stone shaft
Waskada - cairn
Wawanesa - obelisk
Westbourne - obelisk
Winnipeg
   Agricultural College, U of
     M - stele
   Augustine Church - stone
     tablet
   Bank of Montreal - statue
   Brookside Cemetery - cross
   CPR Station - statue
   cenotaph - stone shaft
   East Kildonan - stele
   Elmwood Legion - stone
     block
   Fort Garry - stele
   Fort Rouge Legion - cairn
   44th Battalion - cross
   Kildonan Park - stele

Winnipeg (cont.)
   Medical College, U of M -
     plaque
   Parliament Buildings - Riel
     Statue
   Rebellion Shaft - column
   St. Philip's Church - cairn
   Shaarey Zedek Cemetery -
     stele
   Sir Sam Steele Legion -
     stele
   Soldiers' Relatives - statue
   Ukrainian Cemetery - cross
   Women's Monument -
     statue
Winnipeg Beach - cairn
Winnipegosis - cairn
Woodlands - cairn

NEW BRUNSWICK

Bath - stele and obelisk
Bathurst - obelisk
Burtts Corner - shaft
Campbellton - obelisk
Canterbury - stele
Cap-Pele - slab
Caraquet - slab structure
Chatham - three separate
   blocks
Chipman - stele
Dalhousie - stele
Dorchester - statue
Edmundton - obelisk
Fredericton - shaft
Gagetown - block
Glenwood - stele
Grand Bay - stele
Grand Falls - statue
Grande Anse - cairn
Green Point - cairn
Hampstead & Queenstown -
   stele
Hampton - cairn
Hartland - obelisk
Jacquet River - cairn
McAdam - cairn
Marysville - water fountain
Memramcook - slab
Minto - stele
Moncton - statue
Neguac - slab
Nashwaak Bridge - obelisk
Newcastle
   Anglican Church - cross
   cenotaph - obelisk
New Jerusalem - cairn

Perth-Andover - slabs
Petitcodiac - cairn
Plaster Rock - obelisk
Robertville - stele
Sackville - cross
Saint John
   Boer War - statue
   Cedar Hill Field of Honour
     - cross
   cenotaph - statue
   Jarvis Bay - stele
   Lancaster - stele
St. Leonard - stele
St. Stephen - statue
Shediac - cairn
Southampton - slabs
Stanley - shaft
Sussex - obelisk
Tabusintac - cairn
Tracadie - cairn
Upper Pokemouche - statue
Williamsburg - stele
Woodstock - statue

NEWFOUNDLAND

Badger's Quay - shaft
Bay Bulls - pillar
Bay Roberts - statue
Bonavista
   cemetery - stones
   cenotaph - obelisk
Botwood - obelisk
Brigus - slab
Catalina - obelisk
Charlottetown - tombstone
Clarenville - tombstone
Corner Brook
   Bowater Co. - block
   cenotaph - stone structure
Cupids - cross
Curling - obelisk
Dark Cove - cairn
Deer Lake - arch
Dildo - obelisk
Elliston - obelisk
Gander - statue
Glovertown - shaft
Grand Bank - statue
Greenspond - cross
Harbour Grace - slab
Holyrood - stele
Howley - cross
Jeffrey's - stele
Lamaline - obelisk
Lawn - cairn

Lewisporte - obelisk
New Harbour - stele
Placentia - statue
Port aux Basques
   cenotaph - obelisk
   Caribou sinking
Port Blandford
   WWI - Anglican Church
   WWII - United Church
St. Alban's - stele
St. George's - stele
St. John's
   Bowring Park - caribou and
     Fighting Newfoundlander
   Newfoundland National
     War Memorial - statues
   Pleasantville - cairn
   Sergeants - cross
Spaniard's Bay - shaft
Springdale - shaft
Stephenville - stele
Topsail - shaft
Trinity - shaft
Wabana - stele
Wesleyville - stele
Whitbourne - shaft
Woody Point - cross

NOVA SCOTIA

Amherst - statue
Annapolis Royal - cairn
Antigonish
   cenotaph - obelisk
   WWII - arch
Arcadia - stele
Arichat
Baddeck - stele
Belle Cote - stele
Berwick - stele
Boylston - boulder
Bridgetown - stele
Bridgewater - obelisk
Canning
   Borden Boer War
     Memorial - bust
   cenotaph - stele
Canso - statue
Charlos Cove - cairn
Chester - statue
Cheticamp - stele
Clementsport - cairn
Cole Harbour - natural stone
Dartmouth - cairn
D'Escousse - obelisk
Digby - statue
Donkin - obelisk

Eureka - cairn
Gays River - stele
Glace Bay
   cenotaph - shaft
   Passchendaele Legion
     Branch
Goldboro - cairn
Grand-Etang - obelisk
Guysborough - obelisk
Halifax
   Boer War Fountain, Public
     Gardens - statue
   Boer War Monument,
     Province House - statue
   Bonaventure - anchor
   cenotaph - statue
   Parker-Welsford Memorial,
     Crimean War - arch
   Royal Artillery Park - stele
   Sailor's Memorial - cross
   St. Matthew's Church -
     cross
Hantsport - cairn
Inverness - stele
Judique - statue
Kentville - stele
Kingston - stele
Liscomb - cairn
Liverpool - statue
Lockeport - obelisk
Louisbourg
Lunenburg - statue
Mabou - stele
Mahone Bay - cross
Middle Musquodoboit - statue
Middleton - two plaques
New Glasgow - statue
Newport Corner - cairn
New Waterford - stele
Nine Mile River - two
   tombstone blocks
North Sydney - obelisk
Oxford - statue
Pictou - statue
Port Hood - stele
Port Mouton - cross
Princeville - obelisk
Pugwash - statue
River Bourgeois - stele
River John - stele
St. Peters - cairn
Saulnierville - cairn
Sheet Harbour - cairn
Shelburne - obelisk
Sherbrooke - plaque
Shubenacadie - statue

Springhill - statue
Stellarton - wall
Stewiacke - obelisk
Sydney
   Legion - cross
   Loyal Orange Lodge -
     statue
   Whitney Pier - cairn
Sydney Forks - cairn
Sydney Mines - arch
Tantallon - cairn
Tatamagouche - statue
Thorburn - obelisk
Trenton - statue
Truro - statue
Upper Musquodoboit - blocks
Wallace - stele
Westmount - twin shafts
Westville - statue
Weymouth - cairn
Windsor - shaft
Wolfville - statue
Yarmouth - statue

ONTARIO

Aberfoyle - statue
Acton - stele
Ailsa Craig - cross
Alexandria - cross
Alliston
   Legion - stele
   Public school - stele
Almonte - statue
Alvinston - statue
Amherstburg
   Battle of Pelee Island
   cenotaph - small stele
   Tecumseh's Stone
Angus - cairn
Apsley - block and sphere
Arkona - statue
Arthur - wall
Arnprior - shaft
Athens - cairn
Atikokan
Atwood - statue
Aurora - light tower
Avonmore - obelisk
Aylmer - statue
Ayr - cross
Bancroft - stele
Barrie - shaft with statue
Barry's Bay - stone
   construction
Barwick - obelisk

Bayfield - cairn
Beachville - flagpole
Beamsville - block
Beardmore - cairn
Becher - tombstone
Beeton - gates
Belle River - statues
Belleville
   cenotaph - cross
   Hastings & Prince Edward
    Regiment - stele
Berwick - cairn
Bethany - cairn
Blenheim - gates
Blind River - cairn
Bobcaygeon - chapel
Bolton - statue
Bond Head - gates
Bothwell - stele
Bowmanville - shaft
Bracebridge - shaft
Bradford - stele
Brampton
   cenotaph - stone shaft
   cemetery - cross
Brantford
   Boer War - statue
   cenotaph - stone structure
   Brant Memorial - statue
   IODE monument - stone
    shaft
Brigden - cross
Brighton - pyramid
Brockville
   cenotaph - statue
   Brock Memorial - bust
Bruce Mines - cairn
Burford - cairn
Burks Falls - statue
Burlington - statue
Calabogie
Caledonia - shaft
Callander - stele
Cambridge
   Galt cenotaph - statue
   Hespler cenotaph - stone
    shaft
   Preston cenotaph - statue
   Sons of England - statue
   WREN Memorial - statue
Camlachie - cairn
Campbellford - shaft
Cannington - statue
Cardinal - stele
Carleton Place - stele
Casselman - cross

Cayuga - statue
Charlton - cairn
Chatham
   cenotaph - statue
   Sons of England - stone
    shaft
Chatsworth - standing stone
Chesley - pylon
Chesterville - stele
Chippawa - rough-cut stone
Clinton - stele
Cobalt - concrete structure
Cobourg - cross
Cochrane- cairn
Coe Hill - statue
Colborne - statue
Coldwater - stele
Collingwood - statue
Cookstown - cairn
Cornwall - statue
Corunna - cairn
Craven - shaft
Delaware - two slabs
Delhi - stele
Delta - shaft
Desbarats - stone angel
Deseronto - rough stone
Devlin - cairn
Dixon's Corners - statue
Dorchester - stele
Dresden - plaques
Drumbo - statue
Dryden
   cemetery - cairn
   cenotaph - cairn
Dundas - statue
Dunnville - cross
Durham - statue
Echo Bay - statue
Elgin - cairn
Elmira - statue
Elmvale - cairn
Elora - stele
Embro - shaft
Emo - pyramid cairn
Englehart - obelisk
Espanola - block
Essex - column
Eugenia Falls - statue
Everet - cairn
Exeter
   cenotaph - shaft and globe
   Usborne School - plaque
Fenelon Falls - cross
Fenwick - shaft wall
Fergus - stone slabs

Field - slab
Flesherton - stele
Flinton
Florence - cairn
Fonthill - cross
Forest - statue
Fort Erie
   cenotaph - statue
   Fenian Raid Monument -
    column
Fort Frances - obelisk
Gananoque - statue
Garden River - cairn
Georgetown - statue
Geraldton - stele
Glencoe - stele
Glengarry Tower - pyramid
Goderich
   cenotaph - statue
   Lancaster Bomber #213
Gooderham - block
Grafton - cairn
Grand Bend
   Trench mortar and flagpole
   cemetery - cairn
Grand Valley - shaft
Granton - statue
Gravenhurst - wall
Grimsby - cemetery gate
Guelph
   cenotaph - statue
   CPR station - cross
   Holy Name Society - statue
   Memorial Gardens
   Sons of England - statue
Hagarsville - block
Haileybury - stele
Haliburton - stele
Hamilton
   cenotaph - stone shaft
   St. Paul's Church - cross
Hanover - statue
Harriston - statue
Hastings - stele
Havelock - shaft
Hawkesbury - obelisk
Hearst - cairn
Hensall - statue
Hepworth - cairn
Huttonville - statue
Ilderton - headstone
Ingersol
   cenotaph - flagpole and
    cairn
   cemetery - stone wall
   Sons of England - cross

Ingleside - stele
Iroquois - slabs
Iroquois Falls - obelisk
Jarvis - shaft
Kakabeka Falls - stele
Kapuskasing - stele
Keene - obelisk
Keewatin - cairn
Kemptville - statue
Kenora - statue
Kincardine - cross
Kingston
    cenotaph - cross
    Horse Artillery - stone
        shaft
    Legion Branch No. 9 -
        cairn
    RCAF - stele
    Royal Military College -
        arch
    Signals Corps - statue
    21st Battalion cross and
        statue
Kingsville - cairn
Kintore - statue
Kirkland Lake - obelisk
Kitchener
    cenotaph - stone shaft
    Soldier's Monument - stone
        block
    Bridgeport - stone book
Lakefield - cross
Lancaster - plaque
Larder Lake - pillar
Leamington - stele
Lindsay - statue
Lieury - statue
Lisle - cairn
Listowel - statue
Little Current - statue
London
    Boer War - statue
    Byron - plaque
    cemetery - cross
    cenotaph - stone shaft
    1st Hussars Memorial -
        tank
    Manor Park - statue
    Royal Can. Regiment -
        obelisk
    Univ. of W. Ontario - tower
Longlac - cairn
Lowther - pilon
Lucan - stele
Lucknow - statue
Lyndhurst - obelisk

Marathon - cross
Markdale - stele
Markham - sculpture
Marmora - headstone
Massey - obelisk
Meaford - statue
Medoc - stele
Merrickville - cairn
Midhurst - cairn
Midland - obelisk
Mildmay - stone
Milverton - block
Mitchell - column
Mono Mills - stele
Morewood - statue
Morrisburg
    cenotaph - statue
    Crystler's Farm Battlefield
        - stone shaft
Morton - tombstone
Mount Brydges - statue
Mount Forest - obelisk
Muncey - statue
Napanee - stone urn
New Hamburg - shaft
New Liskeard - cairn
Newbury - cross
Newcastle - stele
Newmarket
    Boer War - bust
    cenotaph - cairn
Newtonville - shaft
Niagara Falls
    cenotaph - statue
    Lundy's Lane Battlefield -
        stone structure
Niagara-on-the-Lake - clock
    tower
Nipigon - slab
North Bay - statue
North Gower - cairn
Norwich - statue
Norwood - stele
Oakland - concrete map of
    Canada
Oakville - stele
Omemee - slab
Orangeville - statue
Orillia - shaft
Oshawa - statue
Ottawa
    Artillery - stone wall
    Boer War - statue
    Canloan Memorial
    City Memorial

Ottawa (cont.)
    Dept. of Vet. Affairs -
        sculpture
    National War Memorial -
        statues
    North West Rebellion -
        statue
    Nurses' Memorial - relief
    RCAF - metal sculpture
    Woman's War Work -
        sculpture
Otterville - cairn
Owen Sound
    cenotaph - stone fountain
    IOOF - cairn
Oxdrift - shaft
Paisley - statue
Palmerston - statue
Paris - cross on wall
Park Hill - cross
Parry Sound - stele
Pembroke - statue
Penetanguishene - cairn
Peterborough
    cenotaph - statues
    North West Rebellion
Petrolia - statue
Pickering - cairn
Picton - statue
Point Edward - column
Poplar Hill - stele
Port Colborne
    cenotaph - stone shaft
    Humberstone - stone
Port Credit - cross
Port Dover - cairn
Port Elgin
    cenotaph - headstone
    Boer War - bust
Port Hope
    cenotaph - statue
    North West Rebellion -
        statue
Portland - stele
Port McNicoll - blocks
Port Rowan - stele
Powassan - stele
Prescott - fountain
Priceville - statue
Queenston
    Brock Monument - column
    cenotaph - statue
    Laura Secord - stone
Rainy River - obelisk
Rannock - statue
Ravenna - statue

Red Rock - cross
Richard's Landing - cairn
Richmond Hill - portico
Ridgetown - shaft
Ridgeway
   cenotaph - stone
   Fenian Raid Memorial -
     cairn
Ripley - block
Rockwood - stele
Roseneath - shaft
St. Catharines
   cenotaph - stone shaft
   Grantham Township -
     shaft
   Legion Branch No. 24 -
     stele
   Merritton - statue
   Merritton Legion - plaque
   North West Rebellion -
     statue
   Polish Legion - stone wall
   Port Dalhousie - statue
   Ukranian - stone shaft
St. George - shaft
St. Joachim - statue
St. Mary's
   cenotaph - statue
   cemetery - cross
St. Thomas
   cenotaph - stele
   Memorial Hospital - statue
St. Williams - cairn
Saltfleet - statue
Sarnia
   Boer War - fountain
   cenotaph - statue
   Sabre Jet
Sault Ste. Marie
   cenotaph - statue
   New Ontario - cairn
Scarborough - large cross
Schomberg - obelisk
Schreiber - obelisk
Seaforth - statue
Shallow Lake - cairn
Shelburne - statue
Simcoe - bell tower
Smiths Falls
   cenotaph - stone shaft
   G.W.V.A. - shaft
   Harvard Trainer
   Memorial Arena - stone
Smithville - cairn
Smooth Rock Falls - stele
Sioux Lookout - obelisk

Southampton - cairn
South Porcupine - cairn
Springfield - cairn
Stirling
Stoney Creek - stone tower
Stouffville - cross
Stratford
   cenotaph - statues
   Perth Regiment - plaque
Strathroy - cross
Stratton - cairn
Streetsville - brick cairn
Sturgeon Falls - cairn
Sudbury - shaft
Sunderland - statue
Teeswater - statue
Temagami - headstone
Terrace Bay - cross
Thamesville
   cenotaph - shaft
   Battle of Thames - cairn
Thedford - cairn
Thessalon - statue
Thornbury - cairn
Thorndale - statue
Thorold
   cenotaph - statue
   Battle of Beaverdams -
     cairn
Thunder Bay
   Fort William - statue
   Port Arthur - stone shaft
Tilbury - gates
Tillsonburg - shaft
Timmins - wall
Tobermory - headstone
Toronto
   Bank of Commerce - arch
   Beaches (Kew Gardens) -
     arch
   Canadian Corps
     Association - statue
   City Hall (Old) cenotaph -
     stone shaft
   City Hall (New) - peace
     garden
   CNE Area
     HMCS Haida
     Lancaster Bomber
     Universal Peace
      Memorial
   East York - stone block
   1812 War Memorial
     (Victoria Park) - bust
   Fitch Memorial (Mount
     Pleasant Cem.) - bust

Toronto (cont.)
   Forest Hill (High School) -
     stone shaft
   Grace Anglican Church -
     column
   Harbord Collegiate
     Memorial - statue
   Hart House (U of T) -
     Soldier's Tower
   Hungarian Freedom
     Fighters - sculpture
   Long Branch Legion -
     building
   Long Branch - cairn
   Malvern Collegiate - statue
   Massey Fergusen Co. -
     cairn (removed)
   Mimicoe - cross
   North York - stone shaft
   Osgoode Hall
     WWI - statue
     WWII - statue
   Polish Monument - stones
   Queen's Own Rifle
     Memorial - cross
   Queen's Park
     Fenian Raids - statues
     48th Highlanders -
      stone shaft
     North West Rebellion -
      statue
   Royal Canadian Yacht Club
     - capstan
   St. Barnabas Anglican
     Church - plaque
   St. James Cathedral - stone
     structure
   Sunnybrook Hospital -
     pylon
   Union Station - CPR
     plaque
   University Avenue
     Boer War - statues
     Edith Cavell - plaque
     RCAF - sculpture
     Sons of England - statue
   York Township - stele
   Weston - stone
Trenton - pillar
Trent River - column
Tweed - stele
Unionville - stone
Uxbridge - statue
Vankleek Hill - post
Victoria Harbour - cross
Vienna - pyramid
Virginiatown - cairn

Walkerton - statue
Wallaceburg - statue
Wardsville
    cenotaph - cairn
    Battle of Longwoods - cairn
Warkworth - stele
Waterford - stele
Waterloo - shaft
Watford - shaft
Waverley - statue
Welland - statues
Wellington - gates
West Lorne - cross
Wheatley - obelisk
Whitby - pylon
Wiarton - statue
Wilton - cairn
Winchester - stele
Windsor
    Boer War - fountain
    cenotaph - stone shaft
    Riverside - cairn
    Sandwich - cairn
Wingham - statue
Woodbridge - tower
Woodstock
    Boer War - bust
    cenotaph - stone wall
    Malcolm MacKenzie -
      obelisk
Wyoming - cairn

PRINCE EDWARD ISLAND
Cardigan - two stelia
Charlottetown
    Boer War - statue
    cenotaph - statues
Cornwall - obelisk and stele
Georgetown - stele
Kensington - stele
Mapleque - statue
Montague - two stelia
Mount Stewart - two stelia
Souris - stele
Summerside - statue
Travellers Rest - obelisk
Tyrone - headstone
Vernon - cross

QUEBEC
Allan's Corner - Battle of
    Châteauguay - obelisk
Asbestos - cross
Ayers Cliff - wall
Beauharnois - stele

Bedford - obelisk
Beebe - gates
Beeton - gates
Bolton Centre - two upright
    stones
Bury - slab
Cap-Sante - plaque
Carillon - pillar
Caughnawaga - shaft
Chambly - statue
Chateauguay - cairn
Chicoutimi - sculpture
Coaticook - stone with plaque
Contrecoeur - plaque
Cookshire - two stones on
    base
Cowansville - stele
Danville
    cenotaph - stone block
    Timothy O'Hae V.C. - cairn
Desbiens
Drummondville - shaft
East Angus - shaft
Farnham - obelisk
Fort Lennox - plaque
Gaspe - statue
Granby
    cenotaph - stone stele
    Boer War - statue
Hatley - slab with plaque
Hemmingford - stele
Howick - stele
Hudson - cairn
Huntingdon - statue
Island Brook - slab
Jacques Cartier - statue
Joliette - sculpture
Knowlton
    cenotaph - statue
    WWII - shaft
Lac Megantic - cairn
Lachute - statue
Lacolle - cairn
La Salle - statue
Lennoxville - obelisk
Levis - cairn
Longueuil - statue
Magog - statue
Maniwaki - stele
Masonville - stone book
Mont-Laurier - shaft
Montmagny - shaft
Montreal
    Bank of Montreal
      Memorial - statue
    Jean Brillant V. C. - stone
      pillar

Montreal (cont.)
    Chénier - statue
    Crémazie - statue
    Dominion Square
        Boer War - statue
        cenotaph - stone shaft
        Crimean War Cannon
    Pierre LeMoyne D'Iberville
      - statue
    Memorial of 1837 Rebellion
      - column
    Nelson's Monument -
      statue
    Notre-Dame-de-Grace -
      sculpture
    Park Lafontaine
        Dollard Memorial -
          statue
        French Memorial - stone
          shaft
    Patriots of 1837 - obelisk
    Scots Guards Memorial -
      obelisk
    Seaman's Memorial - tower
    Windsor Station - CPR
      statue
Montreal West - statue
Mont-St-Michel - headstone
Neuville - plaque
North Hatley - shaft
Ormstown - arch and stele
Outremont - wall
Philipsburg - cairn
Point Claire - cemetery gate
Portage-du-Fort - cairn
Quebec City
    Boer War - statue
    cenotaph - cross
    The Death of Montgomery
      - plaque
    Joan of Arc - statue
    Montcalm - statue
    Montgomery's Army -
      plaque
    Monument des Braves -
      columns
    Wolfe - column
    Wolfe-Montcalm - obelisk
Quyon - obelisk
Rawdon
    cenotaph - stone shaft
    Russian Memorial
Richmond - statue
Rimouski - statue
Riverfield - stele
Rivière du Loup - obelisk

Rock Island - slab
Rouyn-Noranda - obelisk
Ste-Adèle - cairn
Ste-Agathe-des-Monts - obelisk
St-André-Est - plaque
St-Armand - boulder
St-Charles-sur-Richelieu - shaft
St-Denis-sur-Richelieu - statue
St-Hilaire - fountain
St-Hyacinthe - slab
St-Isidne de Laprairie - cairn
St-Jean-sur-Richelieu
    Battle of 6 Sept. 1775 - cairn
    IODE cenotaph - stone block
    No. 48 Infantry Training Centre - stone wall
    22ième Regiment Founding - stone shaft
St-Jérome - cross
St-Lambert - statue
Ste-Marie de Beauce - slabs
Ste-Therese - stele
St-Vincent-de-Paul - stele
Sawyerville - cairn
Scotstown - stone
Shawinigan - stone
Sherbrooke
    cenotaph - statues
    Sherbrooke Fusiliers - tank
Sorel - shaft
South Durham - stele
Stanstead
    cenotaph - cairn
    Stanstead College - gate
    Veteran's plot - stelia
Sutton - plaque
Terrebonne - statue
Thetford Mines - shaft with cross
Trois-Rivières - statue
Ulverton - plaque
Valleyfield
    cenotaph - cairn
    de Salaberry - statue
    Papal Zouaves - statues
Verchères - statue
Victoriaville - cross
Wakefield - headstone
Waterloo - stone with plaque
Westmount - statue
Windsor - shaft

SASKATCHEWAN

Alameda - statue
Arcola - statue
Assiniboia - stone structure
Balcarres - cairn
Batoche - cairn
Battleford
    cenotaph - cairn
    Otter's Camp - cairn
    NWMP cemetery - gate
Bengough - headstone style
Bienfait - cairn
Bjorkdale - shaft
Blaine Lake - obelisk
Brais Corner
Bredenbury - pavillion
Broadview
Canora - stele
Canwood - cairn
Carievale - cairn
Carlyle - tablet
Carnduff - column
Christopher Lake - cairn
Colonsay - cross
Coronach - cairn
Craik
Craven - shaft
Cutbank - pillar
Delisle - cairn
Duck Lake
    Battle of Duke Lake
    cenotaph - cairn
Dundurn - cairn with cross
Elrose - cairn
Esterhazy - cairn
Estevan - obelisk
Fillmore - tablet
Flaxcombe - cairn
Fleming - cairn
Fort Qu'Appelle - tablets
Gainsborough - obelisk
Glaslyn
Glenside - cairn
Glentworth - cairn
Gravelbourg - cairn
Grenfell
Gull Lake - cairn
Herbert - cairn
Humboldt - obelisk
Indian Head - obelisk
Invermay - cairn
Kamsack - shaft
Kennedy - cairn
Kerrobert - cairn
Kincaid - gate

Kindersley
    cemetery - cairn
    cenotaph - cairn
Kinistino - cairn
Kyle - cairn
Lampman - cairn
Landis - cairn
Lashburn - cairn
Lemberg - cairn
Limerick - cairn
Lloydminster - pylon
Lumsden - stone
Mankota - stele
Maple Creek - obelisk
Melfort
Melville - stele
Meyronne - cairn
Midale - cairn
Milden - cairn
Moose Jaw
    cenotaph - cross
    Peacock School - statues
Moosomin - statue
Mossbank - cairn
Nokomis
    Cemetery - gates
    cenotaph - cairn
Norquay - stele
North Battleford
    cemetery - cross
    cenotaph - pylon
    IOOF - sculpture
    Saskatchewan Hospital - sundial
North Portal
Ogema - shaft
Oungre - cairn
Oxbow - arch
Pangman - cairn
Pense - cairn
Piapot - cairn
Prince Albert - statue
Qu'Appelle - cairn
Radville - cairn
Rama - grotto
Readlyn - cairn
Regina
    cemetery - cross
    cenotaph - stone shaft
    28th Battalion - statue
Riverhurst
Rosetown - shaft
Rouleau - statue
Ruddell
Saltcoats - obelisk

Saskatoon
   cenotaph - clock tower
   Hugh Cairns - statue
   Kiwanis Vimy Memorial -
     bandstand
   Next of Kin Memorial -
     avenue of trees
   Univ. of Saskatchewan -
     gate
Shaunavon
Shellbrook - obelisk

Springside
Swift Current - pillar
Tisdale - cairn
Togo - stele
Torquay - cairn
Tramping Lake
Unity - statue
Viceroy - cairn
Wapella - cross
Watrous - shrine
Watson - stones

Weyburn - statue
Whitewood
Willow Bunch - cairn
Windthorst
Wolseley - statue
Woodrow - obelisk
Yorkton - shaft
Young - cairn

YUKON

Dawson - obelisk

OVERSEAS

Canada's war dead are buried in seventy different countries around the world. There are hundreds of cemeteries maintained by the Commonwealth War Graves Commission. Some have familiar names while others are remote and contain only a few graves. The following list represents special memorials in foreign countries that commemorate Canadians. Most were set up by the CWGC.

AFRICA
El Alamein

ASIA
Pusan, Korea - United
   Nations
Rangoon, Burma
Singapore

BELGIUM
Menin Gate
Passchendaele
St. Julien

ENGLAND
Portsmouth Naval
Runnymede
Westminster Abby

FRANCE
Bayeau
Beaumont Hamel
  (Newfoundland)
Bourlon Wood
Courcelette
Courtrai (Newfoundland)
Dieppe

FRANCE (cont.)
Gueudecourt (Newfoundland)
Hill 62
Le Quesnel
Masnieres (Newfoundland)
Vimy Ridge

ITALY
Cassino

NETHERLANDS
Groesbeek

END NOTES

The following short forms have been used:
    PAC - Public Archives of Canada, Ottawa
    DND - Department of National Defense, Ottawa
    PAO - Public Archives of Ontario, Toronto

INTRODUCTION
1. *London Free Press*, 1 June 1925, p. 1.
2. Of the more than 1200 monuments listed in the author's research files (see Appendix B), approximately 66 per cent were built after the First World War and 26 per cent after the Second World War, while only 2 per cent were erected after the Boer War and 6 per cent before that time.
3. Quoted in Heather Robertson, *A Terrible Beauty*, (Toronto: James Lorimer & Co, 1977), p. 92.
4. Memorial File, City Archives, Edmonton, AB.
5. Hodgins Collection, PAO.
6. Smith Collection, Archives of Manitoba, Winnipeg, MB; and Peter Breiger, "Monuments and Their Locations," "Canadian Homes and Gardens", December 1937, p. 50.
7. *Cowichan Leader* (Duncan, BC), 22 February 1978. The application was for a summer-student grant. The repair work went ahead and was sponsored by the local Legion.
8. Donald Webster, ed., *The Book of Canadian Antiques*, (Toronto: McGraw-Hill Ryerson, 1974), p. 9.
9. Allan Ludwig, *Graven Images*, (Middleton, Conn.: Wesleyan University Press, 1966). This book explores the carving on early New England gravestones.
10. William Colgate, *Canadian Art*, (Toronto: Ryerson Press, 1943).
11. Michael Greenwood, "Robert Murray, Against the Monument," *Artscanada*, Autumn 1974, p. 28.
12. Barry Lord, "Siting: The Problem of Art in Architecture," *Artscanada*, October 1969, p. 26.; and Hugo McPherson, "Architecture and Public Art," *Canadian Art*, January-February 1965, p. 20.
13. Al Purdy, *Sex and Death*, (Toronto: McClelland and Stewart, 1973).
14. Erwin Panofsky, ed., *Tomb Sculpture*, (New York: Harry Abrams, 1964), p. 9.

INCENTIVE TO PATRIOTISM
1. Elizabeth Collard, "Nelson in Old Montreal," *Country Life*, July 24, 1969, p. 210.
2. Kathleen Jenkins, *Montreal*, (Garden City, NY: Doubleday & Co, 1966), p. 231.
3. *Ibid.*, p. 253.
4. *Ibid.*, p. 257.
5. Collard, "Nelson in Old Montreal," p. 211.
6. Jenkins, *Montreal*, p. 231.
7. J.C. Dent, *The Last Forty Years*, abridged version with an introduction by Donald Swainson (Toronto: McClelland and Stewart, 1972).
8. J.G. Currie, "The Battle of Queenston Heights," *The Niagara Historical Society Publications*, 4 (1898), p. 35.
9. David B. Read, *Life and Times of General Brock*, (Toronto: W. Briggs, 1894), p. 252.
10. Currie, "The Battle of Queenston Heights," p. 37.
11. Read, *Life and Times of General Brock*, p. 254.
12. Currie, "The Battle of Queenston Heights," p. 37.
13. Read, *Life and Times of General Brock*, p. 257.
14. *Subscription of Various Indian Tribes in Upper Canada in Aid of the Fund for the Reconstruction of Brock's Monument on Queenston Heights*, (Toronto: Queen's Printer, 1841). Copy in the Special Collection, Brock University Library, St. Catharines, ON.

15. J.M.S. Careless, *The Union of the Canadas*, (Toronto: McClelland and Stewart, 1967), pp. 166-69.
16. Betty Minaker, "Brock Monument," (Paper submitted as part of course requirement to Professor Douglas Richardson, University of Toronto, 1978).
17. *British Colonist* (Halifax), December 24, 1859.
18. Hodgins Collection, PAO.
19. Soldiers in various places, including the US during the Civil War, adopted the style of uniform worn by French North African troops called Zouaves. The uniform consisted of loose fitting pants and shirt, a soft cap, and an embroidered vest.
20. *Montreal Star*, June 8, 1881.
21. In June 1981 this statue and the Chénier monument were moved.
22. John Glassco, ed., *The Poetry of French Canada in Translation*, (Toronto: Oxford University Press, 1970), p. 20.
23. DND Records, Guards of Honour for Unveilings, Box 6560, PAC.
24. *Ibid*.
25. *Ibid*.
26. *Montreal Star*, May 25, 1902.
27. James Reaney, *Fourteen Barrels from Sea to Sea*, (Erin, ON: Press Porcepic, 1977), p. 39.
28. Robert B. Nelles, *County of Haldimand*, (Port Hope, ON: Hamly Press, 1905), p. 90.
29. *London Free Press*, March 24, 1909.
30. Bruce Hutchison, *The Incredible Canadian*, (Don Mills, ON: Longman Canada, 1970).
31. W.L. Mackenzie King, *The Secret of Heroism*, (New York, Chicago: F.H. Revell Co., 1906).

CITIZENS OF ALL CLASSES

1. These words are taken from an anonymous story called "The End," which was included in the programme of the unveiling of the memorial in Chatham, Ontario, November 11, 1923. A copy of the programme was sent by Charles Moon of Chatham and is included in the author's research files.
2. This passage comes from an address given by Lieutenant-Colonel D. Sutherland, Minister of Defence, at the dedication of the monument in Galt, Ontario, November 10, 1930. He was quoted in the *Waterloo County Historical Society Annual*, 18 (1930), a copy of which is in the author's files.
3. There is a considerable range in the reporting of American fatal casualty figures for the First World War. The high number of 88 000 is given in A.J.P. Taylor, *The First World War*, (London: H. Hamilton, 1963), while 50 475 is the low estimate quoted by Edward M. Coffman, *The War to End All Wars*, (New York: Oxford University Press, 1968), p. 363. Part of the confusion may come from the inclusion of those who died in the 1918 influenza epidemic.
4. Walter S. Herrington, *War Work of Lennox and Addington*, (Napanee: Beaver Press, 1922), p. 163.
5. DND Records, Applications for Distribution of War Trophies, Box 1205, PAC.
6. These words are taken from the standard inscription used on several monuments erected by the CPR.
7. DND Records, Precedence of Battles and Units, Box 6561, PAC.
8. John Swettenham, *Canada and the First World War*, (Toronto: Ryerson Press, 1969), pp. 75,107, and 109.
9. DND Records, Precedence of Battles and Units, Box 6561, PAC.
10. *Municipal Review* (Montreal), November, 1925.
11. DND Records, Guards of Honour For Unveilings, 1920-1939, Box 6560, PAC.
12. *The Cenotaph, Victory Square*, City Archives, Vancouver, BC.
13. Joseph W. McSpadden, *Famous American Sculptors*, (New York: Dodd, Mead & Co., 1923), p. 269.
14. Herrington, *War Work of Lennox and Addington*, p. 164.
15. From the programme of the memorial unveiling in Chatham, ON, November 11, 1923.
16. *Beeton World*, April 14, 1921.

17. From the programme of the memorial unveiling in Chatham, ON, November 11, 1923.
18. Barbara Wilson, *Ontario and the First World War*, (Toronto: Champlain Society for the Government of Ontario, University of Toronto Press, 1977), p. xxxix.
19. Memorial File, City Archives, Edmonton, AB.
20. Minute Book of the Memorial Committee, Red Deer and District Museum and Archives, Red Deer, AB.
21. *Guelph Daily Mercury*, December 31, 1921.
22. *Souvenir of the Dedication of the Brant War Memorial*, May 25, 1933, copy in the author's research files.
23. DND Records, Memorials, Box 6560, PAC.
24. Charles F. Winter, *Lt. Gen., The Hon. Sir Sam Hughes K.C.B.*, (Toronto: Macmillan of Canada, 1931).
25. Foster Papers, Diary, November 14, 1916, PAC.
26. DND Records, Memorials, Box 6560, PAC.
27. DND Records, Monuments - General, Box 4262, PAC.
28. DND Records, War Trophies and Memorials, Box 4628, PAC.
29. DND Records, Monuments - General, Box 4262, PAC.
30. Regimental Cenotaph, Museum of the Royal Canadian Regiment, London, ON.
31. DND Records, Memorials, Box 6560, PAC.
32. DND Records, War Trophies and Memorials, Box 4628, PAC.
33. DND Records, Monuments - General, Box 4262, PAC.
34. Hodgins Collection, *Report of the Committee of the Ontario Legislature on A Memorial of the Recent War*, March 23, 1921, PAO.

DID YOU LOSE A PAL?

1. The records concerning the Bay of Islands War Memorial are in the possession of Andrew Barrett of Curling, NF. Copies of selected documents are included in the research files of the author.
2. Orr Collection, Perth County Archives, Stratford, ON.
3. Memorial File, City Archives, Edmonton, AB.
4. Minute Book of the Memorial Committee, Red Deer and District Museum and Archives, Red Deer, AB.
5. Newfoundland Historical Society Collection, Monument File, Provincial Archives, St. John's, NF.
6. Robert C. Brown and Ramsey Cook, eds., *Canada - 1896-1921*, (Toronto: McClelland and Stewart, 1974), pp. 232-33.
7. *Globe* (Toronto), May 2, 1925 and May 3, 1932.
8. *Canada Year Book - 1934-35*, (Ottawa: Dominion Bureau of Statistics, King's Printer), p. 365.
9. Mr. Phillip Lohnes's father was the deputy mayor of Mahone Bay, NS, at the time the local monument was built. Mr. Lohnes was the mayor in 1980, and in conversation with the author he thought back to his father's time when the cenotaph was being contemplated and said that "the wealthy people didn't give as much as the poor."
10. *Guelph Daily Mercury*, December 31, 1921.
11. Bay of Islands Memorial documents, author's research files.

THE CONSTANT CLAMOUR

1. Memorial File, City Archives, Edmonton, AB.
2. *Reporter* (Gananoque, ON), November 9, 1977.
3. Northrop Frye, "National Consciousness in Canadian Culture," *Royal Society of Canada Transactions*, 1976, pp. 57-69.
4. *Northern Advance* (Barrie, ON), February 24, 1921.
5. DND Records, Monuments, Box 6560, PAC.
6. *Souvenir of the Dedication of the Brant War Memorial*, May 25, 1933. Copy in the research collection of the author.
7. *Reporter* (Gananoque, ON), November 9, 1977.

8. Memorial File, City Archives, Edmonton, AB.
9. *Daily News* (St. John's, NF), July 2, 1919; and Joy B. Cave, *What Became of Corporal Pittman*, (Portugal Cove, NF: Breakwater Books, 1976).
10. *Northern Advance* (Barrie, ON), December 19, 1918.
11. *Ibid.*
12. From the programme of the memorial unveiling in Chatham, ON, November 11, 1923. A copy of the program is in the author's research files. The population of Chatham according to the 1921 census was 13 256. There were 6439 males. Allowing for the portion of the male population that was too young or too old to be involved in decision making, that 2422 responded positively indicates an overwhelming endorsement.
13. Minute Book of the Memorial Committee, Red Deer and District Museum and Archives, Red Deer, AB.
14. A copy of the Tickell catalogue is located in the DND Records, Monuments - General, Box 4262, PAC, and a copy of the McIntosh Granite Co. catalogue is located in the Orr Collection, Perth County Archives, Stratford, ON.
15. DND Records, Monuments - General, Box 4262, PAC.
16. Memorial File, City Archives, Edmonton, AB.
17. Bay of Islands Memorial documents, author's research files.
18. Rebecca Sisler, *The Girls*, (Toronto: Clarke, Irwin & Co., 1972), pp. 29-30.
19. Minute Book of the Memorial Committee, Red Deer and District Museum and Archives, Red Deer, AB.
20. Board of Assessors' Report, "The Welland War Memorial Competition," *The Journal, Royal Architectural Institute of Canada*, December 1934, p. 182.
21. James Gray, *The Roar of the Twenties*, (Toronto: Macmillan of Canada, 1975), pp. 253-65.
22. DND Records, Applications for Distribution of War Trophies, Box 1205, PAC.
23. Acording to the 1921 census, almost one half of the city's population was Catholic.
24. Public Archives Records, Series IV, Demands for War Trophies, Vol. 9, PAC.
25. John K. Galbraith, *The Scotch*, (Boston: Houghton and Mifflin, 1964), p. 19.
35. *Regina Leader*, November 12, 1926; and *Canadian Annual Review - 1929-30*, (Toronto: Canadian Annual Review Co.), p. 537.

THE WORLD-OLD CUSTOM

1. *Daily Colonist* (Victoria), November 10, 1963.
2. Walter I. Firey, *Land Use in Central Boston*, (Cambridge, Mass.: Harvard University Press, 1947), p. 144. "In this respect the Common illustrates the general principle which Durkheim saw when he observed that man's moral conscience could not long endure without the aid of external reminders. The 'collective conscience' goes through continual variations of intensity, so that it would be liable to extinction during weaker phases unless there were something more enduring to summon it back into being. This need is met by symbols. Moreover, such is the nature of conscience that it cannot be distinctly felt or acted upon without the aid of symbols - what Durkheim calls 'totems.'"
3. Board of Assessors' Report, "The Welland War Memorial Competition," *The Journal, Royal Architectural Institute of Canada*, December 1934, p. 182. "That the monument should, by its form and definite symbolism, clearly indicate its character, this entirely aside from any written inscription."
4. Cecil B. Elliot, "Monuments and Monumentality," *American Institute of Architects Journal*, 41 (1964): 69-71.
5. In the author's files there is information on about 1200 monuments in communities across the country. They break down by type as follows: Stelia and cut-stone constructions - 32 per cent; Statues - 27 per cent; Cairns - 19 per cent; Crosses - 8 per cent; Obelisks - 8 per cent; and Architectural Monuments such as towers - 6 per cent.
6. Cenotaph File, City Archives, Edmonton, AB.
7. In different cultures certain colours and forms can have very different meanings. White rather

than black is the colour of mourning in China. A picture of Mohammed would be unheard of in a Moslem country while pictures of Christ are venerated by many Christians. Monuments, however, are one of the most universally accepted symbols.

8. Graham McInnis, *A Short History of Canadian Art*, (Toronto: Macmillan of Canada, 1939).
9. *Daily Colonist* (Victoria), November 10, 1963.
10. *Toronto Star*, August 23, 1961.
11. *The Telegram* (Toronto), October 22, 1966.
12. *Globe and Mail* (Toronto), April 25, 1961.

SYMBOLIC OF CANADIAN IDEALS

1. H.W. Janson, *History of Art*, (Englewood Cliffs, NJ: Prentice-Hall, 1962), p. 239.
2. Lt.-Col. D.J. Goodspeed, *The Armed Forces of Canada*, (Ottawa: Directorate of History, Canadian Forces Headquarters, 1967), p. 67.
3. *Program for the Annual Memorial Service*, Cartwright, MB, copy in the author's research files.
4. Commissions and Committees, Series D 27, PAO.
5. Roy Ito, *The Japanese Canadians*, (Scarborough, ON: Van Nostrand Reinhold, 1977). According to the number of names listed on the Vancouver memorial, Japanese-Canadian casualties were over twice the national average. Of 195 who served, 54 were killed.
6. James King, *Cleopatra's Needle*, (London: Religious Tract Society, 1893).
7. Shepard B. Clough, *A History of the Western World*, (Boston: D.C. Heath Co., 1967), p. 872.
8. From a caption in the travelling exhibit that appeared at the Art Gallery of Ontario, "Rodin's Sculptural Studies for the monument to 'The Burghers of Calais,'" Cantor-Fitzgerald Group Collection, Toronto, January 27 - March 11, 1979.
9. Monument inscription, St. Lambert, PQ.
10. Margaret Atwood, *Survival*, (Toronto: House of Anansi, 1972), p. 179.
11. Robert Wallace, *The World of Leonardo*, (New York: Time-Life Books, 1966), p. 38.

AT THE MERCY OF PUBLIC TASTE

1. "Hahn and Wife, Sculptors," *Maclean's*, November 19, 1945, p. 19.
2. Hugo MacPherson, "Architecture and Public Art," *Canadian Art*, January-February 1965, p. 20; and Barry Lord, "Siting: the problem of Art in Architecture," *Artscanada*, October 1969, p. 26.
3. "Hahn and Wife, Sculptors," p. 19.
4. Hayward Collection, PAO.
5. Malcolm M. Ross, *The Arts in Canada*, (Toronto: Macmillan of Canada, 1958), p. 58.
6. Letter from the British Business Archives, London, England, copy is in the author's research files.
7. Colin S. MacDonald, *Dictionary of Canadian Artists*, (Ottawa: Canadian Paperbacks, 1967). Much of the biographical information about the artists is taken from this source.
8. Minute Book of the Memorial Committee, Red Deer and District Archives, Red Deer, AB.
9. Hayward Collection, PAO.
10. Joseph W. McSpadden, *Famous American Sculptors*, (New York: Dodd, Mead & Co., 1923), p. 270.
11. Chester File, Cottnam T. Smith, *Some Historical Events of Chester, N.S.*, Public Archives of Nova Scotia, Halifax.
12. The statue of King Edward VII that stands in Toronto's Queen's Park was cast in England and erected originally in India. It was brought to Toronto in the 1960s.
13. MacDonald, *Dictionary of Canadian Artists*.
14. Orr Collection, Perth County Archives, Stratford, ON.
15. *Municipal Review* (Montreal), November, 1925.

CENOTAPH - THE EMPTY TOMB

1. Harry A. Bliss, *Memorial Art*, (Buffalo: Harry A. Bliss, 1912), Introduction.
2. The late Harry Jackman of Toronto.

3. Samuel G. Brandon, *Man and God in Art and Ritual*, (New York: Charles Scribner's, Sons, 1975), p. 22.

4. This is found in a booklet that is in the possession of Clarence Joudry of Mahone Bay, NS.

5. George W. Ferguson, *Sign and Symbol in Christian Art*, (New York: Oxford University Press, 1967), p. 45.

6. Wilfred Owen, "Letter to Sir Osbert Sitwell," quoted on the recording *What Passing Bell*, (London: Decca Records, 1978), a commemoration in poetry and prose of the fiftieth anniversary of the outbreak of the First World War.

7. John Swettenham, *Canada and the First World War*, (Toronto: Ryerson Press, 1969), endpapers.

8. Allan Ludwig, *Graven Images*, (Middleton, CN: Wesleyan University Press, 1966).

9. Erwin Panofsky, ed., *Tomb Sculpture*, (New York: Harry Abrams, 1964) and Kathleen Cohen, *Metamorphosis of a Death Symbol*, (Berkeley: University of California Press, 1973).

10. A.B. Hickson is the writer of the Summerside inscription.

NOTHING ON WHICH TO FOUND A COUNTRY

1. *Age Dispatch* (Strathroy, ON), August 28, 1924.

2. DND, War Trophies Register, PAC.

3. Public Archives Records, Requests for War Trophies, PAC.

4. DND Records, War Trophies Register, PAC.

5. DND Records, War Trophies and Memorials, Box 4628, PAC.

6. Smaller and more remote communities often used the war trophies as integral parts of their monuments. This was probably because they couldn't afford statues or other expensive memorials. It is in a few of these places that the guns can still be found.

7. The Second World War resulted in very little desire for war trophies in Canada.

8. City Council Minutes, October 18, 1982, St. Catharines Historical Museum, St. Catharines, ON.

9. Grant Application File, Ontario Heritage Foundation, Toronto.

10. Portage du Fort, PQ, and Newtonville, ON, were two places where older monuments were adapted for use as memorials to the First World War. The one in Portage du Fort had been built in the late 1850s to mark the visit to the area of the Lieutenant-Governor's wife, Lady Head. The memorial in Newtonville originally commemorated the one man from the town who had been killed in the Boer War; Nicholas Gage, *Portrait of Greece*, (New York: American Heritage Press, 1971), p. 126. The author talks abut ancient shrines being used by new religions.

12. Alden Nowlan, "Ypres: 1915," *15 Canadian Poets*, (Toronto: Oxford University Press, 1970), p. 124.

SELECTED BIBLIOGRAPHY

Books or articles that say something specific about a monument or monuments in Canada, or that say something significant about memorials in general, have been included in this source list. Accessibility has also been a consideration.

Bliss, Harry A. "Introduction," *Memorial Art.* Buffalo: Harry A. Bliss, 1912.

Brandon, Samuel G. *Man and God in Art and Ritual.* New York: Charles Scribner & Sons, 1975.

Breiger, Peter. "Monuments and Their Locations," *Canadian Homes and Gardens,* December 1937.

Brown, Robert C. and Ramsey Cook, eds. *Canada – 1986-1921.* Toronto: McClelland and Stewart, 1974.

Careless, J.M.S. *The Union of the Canadas.* Toronto: McClelland and Stewart, 1967.

Cohen, Kathleen. *Metamorphosis of a Death Symbol.* Berkeley: University of California Press, 1973.

Collard, Elizabeth. "Nelson in Old Montreal," *Country Life,* 24 July 1969.

Correspondence, Addresses etc. connected with the Subscription of Various Indian Tribes in Upper Canada in Aid of the Fund for the Reconstruction of Brock's Monument on Queenston Heights. Toronto: Queen's Printer, 1841.

Currie, J.G. "The Battle of Queenston Heights," *The Niagara Historical Society Publications.* 4, 1898.

Dent, J.C. *The Last Forty Years,* abridged version with an introduction by Donald Swainson. Toronto: McClelland and Stewart, 1972.

Elliot, Cecil B. "Monuments and Monumentality," *American Institute of Architects Journal.* 41, 1964.

Ferguson, George W. *Sign and Symbol in Christian Art.* New York: Oxford University Press, 1967.

Firey, Walter L. *Land Use in Central Boston.* Cambridge, MS: Harvard University Press, 1974.

Frye, Northrop. "National Consciousness in Canadian Culture," *Royal Society of Canada Transactions,* 1976.

Goodspeed, Lt. Col. D.J. *The Armed Forces of Canada.* Ottawa: Directorate of History, Canadian Forces Headquarters, 1967.

Gray, James. *The Roar of the Twenties.* Toronto: Macmillan of Canada, 1975.

Greenwood, Michael. "Robert Murray, Against the Monument," *Artscanada,* Autumn 1974.

Herrington, Walter S. *War Work of Lennox and Addington.* Napanee: Beaver Press, 1922.

Janson, H.W. *History of Art.* Englewood Cliffs, N.J.: Prentice-Hall, 1962.

Journal, The. Royal Architectural Institute of Canada, December 1934.

Lord, Barry. "Siting: The Problem of Art in Architecture," *Artscanada,* October, 1969.

Ludwig, Allan. *Graven Images.* Middleton, CN: Wesleyan University Press, 1966.

MacDonald, Colin S. *Dictionary of Canadian Artists.* Ottawa: Canadian Paperbacks, 1967.

Maclean's. 19 November 1945.

McInnis, Graham. *A Short History of Canadian Art.* Toronto: Macmillan of Canada, 1939.

McPherson, Hugo. "Architecture and Public Art," *Canadian Art.* January-February, 1965.

McSpadden, Joseph W. *Famous American Sculptors.* New York: Dodd, Mead & Co., 1923.

Municipal Review. Montreal, November 1925.

Panofsky, Erwin, ed. *Tomb Sculpture.* New York: Harry Abrams, 1964.

Robertson, Heather. *A Terrible Beauty.* Toronto: James Lorimer & Co. 1977.

Ross, Malcolm M. *The Arts in Canada.* Toronto: Macmillan of Canada, 1958.

Sisler, Rebecca. *The Girls.* Toronto: Clarke, Irwin & Co., 1972.

Swettenham, John. *Canada and the First World War.* Toronto: Ryerson Press, 1969.

Wilson, Barbara. *Ontario and the First World War.* Toronto: Champlain Society for the Government of Ontario, University of Toronto Press, 1977.

Wood, Herbert Fairlic and John Swettenham. *Silent Witness.* Toronto: Hakkert, 1974.

INDEX